"Rick Cornish, with his 100 essays, makes it easy for us to keep God's Word on our hearts daily and gives us the tools to discuss the deep things of God."

—STEVE LARGENT

former U.S. Congressman from Oklahoma;
member, NFL Hall of Fame

"I have found these readings to be clear, accurate, well-chosen, and personally stimulating, covering the topics appropriately. I highly recommend this book."

—CRAIG BLOMBERG

distinguished professor of New Testament, Denver Seminary

"Spirituality without understanding is not faith; it is superstition. In *5 Minute Theologian,* Rick Cornish serves up reader-friendly and character enriching insights. I strongly recommend these highlights of classical Christianity. I want to send copies to my children and grandchildren!"

—GORDON R. LEWIS, PH.D.

author, *Decide for Yourself;* coauthor, *Integrative Theology*

5

MINUTE
Theologian

MAXIMUM TRUTH
IN MINIMUM TIME

RICK CORNISH

OUR GUARANTEE TO YOU

We believe so strongly in the message of our books that we are
making this quality guarantee to you. If for any reason you are
disappointed with the content of this book, return the title page
to us with your name and address and we will refund to you the
list price of the book. To help us serve you better, please briefly
describe why you were disappointed. Mail your refund request
to: NavPress, P.O. Box 35002, Colorado Springs, CO 80935.

For a free catalog
of NavPress books & Bible studies call
1-800-366-7788 (USA) or 1-800-839-4769 (Canada).

www.navpress.com

The Navigators is an international Christian organization. Our mission is to advance the
gospel of Jesus and His kingdom into the nations through spiritual generations of
laborers living and discipling among the lost. We see a vital movement of the gospel,
fueled by prevailing prayer, flowing freely through relational networks and out into the
nations where workers for the kingdom are next door to everywhere.

NavPress is the publishing ministry of The Navigators. The mission of NavPress is to
reach, disciple, and equip people to know Christ and make Him known by publishing
life-related materials that are biblically rooted and culturally relevant. Our vision is to
stimulate spiritual transformation through every product we publish.

NAVPRESS and the NAVPRESS logo are registered trademarks of NavPress. Absence of
® in connection with marks of NavPress or other parties does not indicate an absence of
registration of those marks.

ISBN 1-57683-483-2

Cover Design: Arvid Wallen
Creative Team: Don Simpson, Rachelle Gardner, Arvid Wallen
        Darla Hightower, Glynese Northam

Unless otherwise identified, all Scripture quotations in this publication are taken from
the HOLY BIBLE: NEW INTERNATIONAL VERSION® (NIV®). Copyright © 1973, 1978,
1984 by International Bible Society. Used by permission of Zondervan Publishing
House. All rights reserved. Other versions include: the *Revised Standard Version Bible*
(RSV), copyright 1946, 1952, 1971, by the Division of Christian Education of the
National Council of the Churches of Christ in the USA, used by permission, all rights
reserved; and the *New King James Version* (NKJV). Copyright © 1982 by Thomas Nelson,
Inc. Used by permission. All rights reserved.

Library of Congress Cataloging-in-Publication Data
Cornish, Rick, 1950-
  5 minute theologian : maximum truth in minimum time / Rick
Cornish.
    p. cm.
Includes bibliographical references.
  ISBN 1-57683-483-2
  1. Baptists--Doctrines. I. Title.
  BX6331.3.C67 2004
  230--dc22
                                    2003022053

Printed in the United States of America
3 4 5 6 7 8 9 10 11 / 11 10 09 08

To my sons, Scott and Ben, and their wives,
whom I do not yet know, and their children,
who have not yet been born.
"Be transformed by the renewing of your
mind." (Romans 12:2)

Contents

Foreword

Christian theology historically has been known as the "queen of the sciences." As such, it has occupied a prominent place among the classical disciplines of learning. A great preacher of our day has said that theology is akin to a referee at a basketball game. He is hardly seen but controls all that goes on. Like the referee, theology is not often visible, but it controls all the Christian's thinking, values, and actions. But theology, which has played so central a role in Christian faith and living through the centuries, is sadly neglected in our day. In our postmodern culture, many of us are more fascinated with our feelings and more energized by our activities than by core Christian truth. Many barely recognize that Christian theology is a foundation without which the structure of our faith collapses.

As a missionary in Africa, I observed the church there growing explosively. Millions of people have come to Christ in recent decades. When thoughtful church leaders were asked to identify the African church's greatest need, they replied, "To be grounded in Christian theology." Many new converts, sincerely searching but ignorant of essential Christian truths, have drifted into seductive cults. Widespread ignorance of the Christian faith is also pervasive in the so-called "enlightened" West. Recent research shows that 85 percent of Americans call themselves Christians, but a shocking number of saints think that the Bible is not accurate, Jesus sinned, the Devil is not a personal being, and hell is a myth. God through the prophet warns, "My people are destroyed from lack of knowledge" (Hosea 4:6).

Here's where *5 Minute Theologian* fills a serious need, by offering one hundred capsule explanations of essential Christian beliefs. Don't allow the title to deceive you into thinking this is "Christianity Lite." It reflects solid understanding of Christian theology and the positions of leading theologians from our Christian heritage. *5 Minute Theologian* is sophisticated theology presented in easily digested, bite-sized portions. The chapters are short, but packed with substance. The material is simplified, but not simplistic. It represents a marvelous resource for the entire family to read, discuss, process, and apply. Thoughtfully read this faithful and stirring work by Pastor Rick Cornish and you, like I, will break out into the Doxology if not the Hallelujah Chorus!

BRUCE DEMAREST, PH.D.
Professor of Theology & Spiritual Formation
Denver Seminary, Denver, Colorado

Acknowledgments

As is true of every book, many people contributed to this one. In addition to listening to me read these essays, my wife Tracy and my sons Scott and Ben gave up many hours with husband and father that I might pursue this project. Don Simpson, Rachelle Gardner, Darla Hightower, Glynese Northam, and Nicci Jordan of NavPress provided expert guidance throughout the writing and publication process.

Rhonda Morris, my office administrator, read the entire manuscript, making valuable suggestions throughout. The board and people of First Baptist Church in Luverne, Minnesota, shared their pastor with this book. The youth group and parents of Fellowship Bible Church in Tulsa, Oklahoma, tested the essays' suitability for teen readers.

This book would not have been written without the encouragement of Drs. Bruce Demarest, Ken Gangel, Craig Blomberg, Gordon Lewis, Bob Osburn, and NFL Hall-of-Famer and former U.S. Congressman Steve Largent. The first to urge me to write this book were Janice David and Joe Seelig.

Introduction

I once met a woman who claimed to be a communist, so I started asking her to explain why she thought communism was the way to go. She grew flustered and defensive, but wasn't able to answer my questions or support her view. It turned out she didn't know even the basics of Marxism. I concluded she wasn't much of a communist, if she was one at all. I thought, *How sad to declare belief in a system, but reveal such ignorance of it!* Then it hit me that countless Christians are similar—claiming to believe something we know little about. Wouldn't it make others wonder if we're really Christians—or even make them question the validity of Christianity itself?

Jesus said, "Love the Lord your God with all your heart and with all your soul and with all your *mind*" (Matthew 22:37). Historically, Christianity has been a thinking faith. Ordinary Christians like you and me were deeply concerned about the depth and details of Christian doctrine, desiring to love God with their minds, first and foremost. Today, many Christians are content to love God with heart and soul, leaving their minds out of it. My desire is to help Christians love the Lord with all we have—including our minds—which starts with learning the theology of the Bible.

Church history can be very convicting. Consider the scene in Alexandria, Egypt, in A.D. 318. Christians nearly rioted in the streets over a doctrinal dispute about the person and nature of Christ. Can you imagine such theological frenzy today in Minneapolis or Denver or Tulsa? From our more immediate heritage, I think of Puritan New England, perhaps the most intellectual community the world has known. The people in the pew demanded first-rate scholarship from their pastors in the pulpit—and they got it.

Today, pastors see a great gulf between our thinking class—scholars who pursue deep Christian truths—and believers in the pew who are divorced from knowledge or even hold it in disdain. Many Christians seem to believe that as long as our scholars think about theology, the rest of us are safe from sinking into heresy. Our pastors will anchor us, holding us to the rock of divine revelation. This belief implies that it doesn't matter if the rest of us drift with "every wind of teaching and . . . the cunning and craftiness of men in their deceitful scheming" (Ephesians 4:14). But each of us is accountable for our own spiritual development, and the best preachers, teachers, and theologians in the world can't protect us if we don't arm ourselves with the "sword of the Spirit, which is the word of God" (Ephesians 6:17).

Compared to the past, few churches today really teach the Bible. Much contemporary preaching and writing accommodates Christianity to "me and my world," applying Scripture to our personal needs without first making sure we understand it. Application is essential, but it can be overemphasized if people never learn the truth they should apply. We cannot live "Christianly" without knowing Christianity, any more than we can build a bridge without knowing engineering. We can't apply what we don't know.

If we don't learn the theology of the Bible, we invite several catastrophic results. First, we leave ourselves exposed, vulnerable to attack by unbelievers who want to win us to their pagan beliefs. Second, we cannot defend our faith against the philosophers of this age who are eager and ready to go to war against Christianity. Third, we cannot adequately explain the gospel to seekers who genuinely inquire about our faith.

For any truth system to survive, its adherents must know its foundational beliefs—the basic tenets upon which it stands. If Christians don't maintain a grasp on these, can we expect Christianity to withstand the onslaughts of this fallen world? Do we anticipate that it will thrive without our efforts to defend and promote it? Or do we think that's the Holy Spirit's job; we can be passive and He'll make up the slack?

Indeed, the Spirit does His job even if we don't do ours. But to indirectly use the Spirit as an excuse for our theological ignorance is not what He intends or wants. For all the Spirit's influence in and through us, our system of truth is still that—a system as opposed to chaos, and truth as opposed to falsehood. Knowledge is thus required, and knowledge is the fruit of study. As someone has said, "The Spirit was not given to make study unnecessary, but to make study effective."

If I could establish a must-read list for Christians, I would rank near the top J. P. Moreland's excellent book *Love Your God with All Your Mind* (1997, NavPress). He brings the matter home by asking: How can a person faithfully attend an evangelical church for decades and still know next to nothing about the teaching and history of Christianity? It's a big problem and I've written *5 Minute Theologian* to try to be part of the solution.

If we think it doesn't matter, recall that it takes only one generation of ignorance for truth to die. If we neglect Christian teaching, Christianity may be only a memory to our grandchildren. Even now, if unbelievers realized the level of our theological ignorance, would they conclude that we're already no longer Christian?

I need constant reminders that in a fallen, unstable world, only God's Word endures. God recently reminded me of that when my wife Tracy and I learned that she has ovarian cancer with a 50-50 chance of even being alive in five years. Isaiah was right: "The grass withers and the flowers fall, but the word of our God stands forever" (Isaiah 40:8). If she and I don't know the truth of the Rock upon which we stand, we'd better learn now!

Our family faces anew the sobering question of the reality of our faith. Will it sustain us as we ponder the possibility of Tracy going to heaven earlier than we expected? She may still live to be ninety, but we know in a new way that anticipated longevity can vanish in one doctor's visit. Our faith will have little chance of doing its job if we're ignorant of its content. When the pressures of life explode into catastrophe, will our faith fail us? It surely will if we don't know it.

Our safe and prosperous Western culture draws us in, making us after its own image. But transformation away from the world and into God's mold is possible. Paul commanded such transformation and instructed us how to attain it. "Do not conform any longer to the pattern of this world, but be transformed by *the renewing of your mind*" (Romans 12:2, emphasis added). The means of a transformed life is a renewed mind—a mind shaped by God's revealed truth in Scripture. The ongoing process of renewing our minds begins with learning the theological basics from the Bible, then allowing ourselves to be shaped by what we learn as we apply it to life.

Paul's warning to Timothy seems ominously prophetic of our day: "The time will come when men will not put up with sound doctrine. Instead, to suit their own desires, they will gather around them a great number of teachers to say what their itching ears want to hear" (2 Timothy 4:3). But Paul's simple, direct command to Titus should still be the pastor's guide: "You must teach what is in accord with sound doctrine" (Titus 2:1). I believe the best way to achieve that in the pulpit is for people in the pew (most of you reading this book) to demand it as they did in Puritan New England.

Wonderful theologies have been written, but few believers buy and read and study them. At the other end of the spectrum, devotionals abound, but how many provide long-term learning benefit? The aim of 5 Minute Theologian is to partially bridge the gap, summarizing basic theological topics for those inquisitive enough to want more than a devotional, but not ready for heavy-duty theology. My hope is that this book will be an understandable primer, written in short sections for busy people, for those who want to proceed on the journey between minimal learning and serious study.

My first reason for writing 5 Minute Theologian originated from my role as a dad reading to my sons, Scott and Ben, to develop their spiritual growth and prepare them for life as thinking Christians. I found that Christian bookstores carry many light, self-oriented books for teens, but few of substance between the "kid's stuff" and college level sources. So I started preparing my own daily readings. Other parents of Christian teens asked for copies, and eventually they grew into this book.

The second reason came from my experience as a college teacher at a Christian university in the former Soviet Union. What an eye-opener! The typical Christian student from Russia or Ukraine, even with limited opportunity for religious training, is far more theologically aware than the average American Christian student. Compounding the problem, few colleges and universities in the West are intellectually or spiritually conducive to Christianity or Christians. Some professors are determined to rid "gullible" freshman of "religious mythology," usually meaning Christianity. We need to do a better job of preparing our Christian young people for the intellectual and spiritual battles ahead.

My third reason emerged from my ministry as a pastor. I have observed the lack of theological understanding among people in American churches. As has often been said, Western Christianity is a mile wide but an inch deep. Os Guinness writes that the church in America has more people, money, and other resources than the church in any time or place in history, but less impact. Yes, he's talking about us. And Jesus told us that to whom much is given, much is required (Luke 12:48). The clash between Guinness's observation and Jesus' comment alarms me, and should alarm us all.

My initial audience was high school-age believers, but since inquisitive Christians come in all age groups, I hope this book will serve a wider spectrum. I am primarily aiming for spiritually motivated Christians who want to learn and grow in the faith. This book is not written for believers who need their spiritual furnace stoked— other books will serve them better.

I have found that thinking Christians are excited about learning, and everyone has time for five minutes of focused thought each day. I have tried to make these brief minutes count by communicating maximum truth in minimum time. The essays are not detailed, but contain condensed versions of the main points of Christian theology. *5 Minute Theologian* is intended to supplement, not replace, Bible reading and study. The essays can be read and the verses studied and cross-referenced to explore the topics further.

I hope parents will use *5 Minute Theologian* to ground their kids in basic Christian truth. It can also function as a reference for high school graduates heading to college as well as serve as curriculum for youth groups, Christian schools, and homeschoolers.

The parts of the book are ordered in one of the common arrangements of many theology books. Part 1 introduces theology, the process of thinking about theology, and issues related to studying theology. The raw material of our theology, the Bible, is considered in part 2. Part 3 discusses God, the source of all truth and all that is. Mankind, who we are, and what we're like, enters the picture in part 4. Part 5 deals with sin, which explains why we find ourselves in the dilemma we're in. Christ, the solution to our sin and its consequences, is the subject of part 6. Part 7 develops the glorious doctrines of salvation—what God has done on our behalf. The Holy Spirit and His ministry is the topic of part 8. Part 9 considers the church, the corporate expression of God's people. Part 10 covers last things, both individually and collectively.

I hope that *5 Minute Theologian* will provide daily readings of substance for Christians who want more than a devotional. If it helps bridge the gap between shallow, trendy Christianity and a deeper, more historic Christian faith, it will have served its purpose.

NATURAL THEOLOGIANS

Born to Think

Who am I and why am I here? What's the purpose of life? What's real, true, right, good? If God exists, what is He/She/It like, and how would I know? Might God have anything to do with me, and how would He tell me? Why do people suffer and die, and what happens next? These theological topics crisscross the landscape of a person's soul.

People often think theology is boring. But the title, not the topic, bores them. The word "theology" suffers from bad press. Most people, by their inquisitiveness, are natural theologians. A theologian must be curious, an asker of big questions—and by that definition, most of us could be called theologians.

In truth, almost everyone ponders those big questions and their possible answers. Such activity is central to a human being's inner world, whether formulated in lofty language, or expressed in common lingo, or never spoken out loud. So even though few of us ask, "Should I or should I not be a theologian?" we all live the result of being theologians.

Christian theology studies the big questions and issues, taking its name from the biggest—God. It studies God and everything related to God: the world; human beings, including ourselves and our problems; our lack of relationship with God and how to have one; truth and falsehood; right and wrong; the Bible; Jesus; the Holy Spirit; Satan and angels; the church; the future. Almost everything fits somewhere in the theological grid, even though we may not think of it as "theology."

Theology teaches us what Christianity believes and how to live. By knowing and applying theology, we make wise decisions and take godly actions. Theology explains the "whys" behind God's commands and prohibitions. Thus, our daily lives and our spiritual growth are connected to our learning and living theology. It's not surprising that Jesus included the mind in the greatest commandment about loving God (Matthew 22:37). To not apply our God-given minds to the study of theology is to disobey the Lord's command. On the other hand, to obey the Lord's command by applying our minds to His truth is to please God.

Without reasoned, coherent answers to our big questions, life makes no sense. Outside of theology, we cannot find relevance. All other pursuits result in dead ends. If our questions are left unanswered, nothing seems to fit in life, or even in our thoughts. Everything remains unanchored, floating in midair. Without theology, life leads to despair—in extreme cases, to suicide. So theology, rather than being irrelevant, is the foundation of all relevance.

Why Study Theology?

In our day, theology is often denounced as irrelevant, unnecessary, or outdated. Polls reveal an alarming and growing opposition to theology. Even Christians rate theological knowledge last on the list of pastoral qualifications. For some people, theology is only rules and legalism; for others it's mere philosophy divorced from everyday life.

"Can't I just read the Bible, have faith, and love Jesus? Why study theology?" Such questions reveal a common misunderstanding about theology, even a bias against it. Reading the Bible, having faith, and loving Jesus all require thinking and understanding. Theology explains our reading of the Bible, builds our faith, and increases our love of Jesus. These tasks cannot be adequately done without thinking and theology.

"Theology" comes from two Greek words, which mean "God" and "word, discourse, thinking, or reflecting." Together, in simple terms, they mean thinking about and discussing God and related subjects such as the Bible, faith, Jesus, and other big questions about truth and life and reality. The ancient Greek philosopher Aristotle considered theology the greatest discipline because its main object of study, God, is the highest reality. Even into the Middle Ages, theology was known as "The Queen of the Sciences."

In past centuries, and even today, some people divorced theology from the Bible, considering it an independent field of study. But Christian theology cannot be separated from the Bible. It is essentially studying the Bible by topic, rather than in the order the text appears. Theology looks at the Bible's teaching on a subject in all the passages where that subject appears; exposition is the study of the Bible's passages in verse-by-verse order, regardless of the topics in those verses. The two processes go together.

Theology relates to two themes—truth and life. It helps us understand and organize God's truth in Scripture and advises how to live in light of that truth. Theology uncovers the universal biblical principles we can apply to our lives. Without it, Christianity is reduced to a folk religion—familiar and reassuring but unrelated to real life. Christians are then unprepared to face the media blitz of secularization and the influences of cultic falsehoods. Without understanding of the truth, our worship diminishes into tradition, our beliefs degenerate into legalism or heresy, our desire for spirituality may pursue nonChristian paths, and our lives become devoid of service to God and others.

In addition to theology's practical relevance, Jesus commanded us to love God with our *minds* (Matthew 22:37; Mark 12:30; Luke 10:27). Yes, we glorify God by godly living, but godly living proceeds from godly thinking, including the study of theology. Lazy and irrational thinking does not glorify God. A real lover of God and disciple of Jesus develops and uses the mind.

You may not think of yourself as a theologian, and you may not practice theology in a formal setting like a seminary. But everyone who thinks is a theologian, for at times, we all ponder God and the big questions of truth, life, and reality.

WHICH THEOLOGY?

Who Has It Right?

The inevitable follow-up question to "Why study theology?" is "Which theology?" Throughout its history, the church has devised too many theologies to mention. In addition to the many classic options, new ones spring up continually. So we should clarify which theology we mean when we encourage people to study it.

First, we are talking about Christian, rather than nonChristian, theology. The world's other major religions organize their beliefs according to a certain structure, as Christians do. But their belief systems lie outside the scope of this book.

Second, our focus will be Protestant rather than Roman Catholic theology. This distinction does not suggest that we believe Roman Catholics have nothing to offer. It does reflect major differences between the two. The most fundamental disagreement is on the locus of authority. Protestants believe authority resides in Scripture alone. Roman Catholics find it in church tradition as expressed by church councils and the pope, in addition to the Bible. Most other doctrinal variations between these two major branches of Christianity stem from this issue.

Third, within Protestantism, for purposes of this book we'll express evangelical rather than liberal theology. Perhaps the most significant evangelical distinctive, especially in America, is belief in the historic doctrines of the faith found in Scripture. Liberal theology largely rejects them or redefines them in novel ways, often due to placing supreme confidence in human reason rather than divine revelation. Cut loose from the secure anchor of Scripture, liberalism changes with each cultural season.

But what about differences within Protestantism, or even within Evangelicalism? Various denominations emphasize some doctrines above others and more than other groups do. For instance, Baptists usually emphasize baptism, specifically by immersion, more than other doctrines. Many Presbyterians stress God's sovereignty more than other Christians do. Charismatics highlight the Holy Spirit and His role in our lives. Denominations originally arose in part out of these doctrinal emphases, and many of those distinctions continue today.

Evangelicals agree on the following major doctrines: the inspiration of Scripture; the triune God existing as the Father, the Son, and the Holy Spirit; the deity of the Son and the Spirit as well as the personality of the Spirit;

the created goodness but fallen sinfulness of mankind; salvation by grace alone received through faith alone because of Christ alone; the bodily resurrection and return of Christ. Differences among evangelicals include issues related to predestination, church government, spiritual gifts, and the end times.

Most evangelicals believe we can debate without dividing. The evangelical spirit leans toward flexible cooperation, a significant change from our fundamentalist forebears. One challenge within Evangelicalism is finding the right degree of flexibility. While escaping the harshness of narrow extremism in one direction, we must avoid giving away the doctrinal farm in the opposite direction. Most evangelicals agree with this concept, but may disagree over where the boundary is found.

The intent of this book is to summarize Christian theology from the evangelical Protestant view — my own perspective. As is true of everyone, I cannot claim perfect objectivity, but I will try to alert the reader to debated points as well as portray other views fairly and accurately.

A Process for Studying Theology

Theology seems a daunting field for even the sharpest thinker. So many texts and topics clutter the mind that we barely know how to begin. Even with the Holy Spirit's help we need a process to guide our efforts. Our method should lead to conclusions based on solid evidence—conclusions that don't contradict one another and are honestly believable.

Bruce Demarest and Gordon Lewis propose the following six-step plan.[1] Their approach was initially designed for serious research, but the principles benefit even casual study. One does not need to be formally trained to profit from incorporating these step-by-step guidelines.

1. Define the problem or topic. Precisely what is the issue you are examining? You can't do serious investigation if you don't know what you're looking for. People often argue over a theological issue when they haven't clearly defined the point under discussion. They might

even agree, but not be aware of it. Or they might disagree, but not be aware of that. Without defining the topic, they can't know if they're even talking about the same thing.

2. *Learn alternative views.* What did godly scholars throughout church history discover? Remember, the indwelling Holy Spirit assisted them as well as us. We may not always agree with our spiritual ancestors' conclusions, but we would be arrogant not to consider the results of their work.

3. *Investigate the Bible's teaching on the topic.* This step explores the raw material of Christian theology. It requires sound interpretation and should review all the relevant passages. Using only isolated verses may result in an incomplete or even distorted understanding of the Bible's teaching. This step includes reconciling verses that seem to say contrary things.

4. *Form a cohesive doctrine.* Based on the biblical data, summarize your findings in a systematic manner. This doctrinal conclusion should not contradict other biblical doctrines or true knowledge from other fields. If it does, dig deeper and think better.

5. *Defend your doctrine.* Consider its validity in the light of other options. Can it withstand objections from philosophy, science, different theologies, religions, and

cults? If not, it needs more work. This step will continue as new challenges confront Christianity.

6. *Apply your conclusions to life and ministry.* Put into practice what you believe. Our study should not lead to mere theoretical ideas, but should make a difference in our lives and those we meet. From start to finish our incentive should surpass merely accumulating facts. The development of inner character and its expression in outer action should be our goal.

This process may seem intimidating. But it's not designed to be followed step-by-step every time we open the Bible. It does, however, offer a framework for study over the long haul, and its principles guard our theology from faulty methods even in daily reading.

EPISTEMOLOGY

What, How, and Whom Do We Know?

"It's not what you know, but who you know that counts." Depending on the context, that well-known saying may or may not be true. But each side of the saying includes the same factor—knowledge. Our culture increasingly prefers feelings to knowledge, but we cannot live without knowledge. So where do we begin learning about knowing?

If we limit that question to theology, theologians pose three starting points.

1. Some start with mankind—our concerns and questions—then go to the Bible for answers. But those theologies reflect only the issues and perspectives of their own age and culture.

2. Since God is the ultimate reality some theologies start with Him—the part called Theology Proper.

3. Others begin with the source of knowledge about God—the Bible. This division of theology is called Bibliology. We will start with number three in this book.

But even before we begin our theology, we face a preliminary issue—how we learn and think at all. What is knowledge, and how do we learn it? The most common theories about learning truth are called rationalism and empiricism. Rationalism believes that knowledge originates in the human mind. Its emphasis on thinking and ideas is the hallmark of the philosopher. But rationalism is limited because it assumes that our minds have the potential to know everything. As a result, any knowledge that might exist outside our minds remains unexplored. Rationalism refuses to pioneer the unknown.

Empiricism believes that knowledge begins with the senses—what we see, hear, feel, taste, and touch. This approach is the method of the scientist who conducts experiments and observes the results as a basis for knowledge. But this method is also limited because experiments cannot reproduce events from the past or beyond our realm in the present. Those areas are untouchable to empiricism and remain a mystery. Empiricism is content to stay within the limitations of human experience.

Rationalism and empiricism are good and necessary tools for living, but deficient for exploring questions of ultimate truth. Both presume knowledge based on the assumption that truth exists only within the limitations of our human capacities. But can we say no truth exists outside us? If truth does exist outside, we can know it only if it's revealed by something or Someone also on the outside. That's what Christians believe—God exists outside the box of our awareness, and He has penetrated inside to reveal Himself to us.

So Who we know is crucial in our search for knowledge. To know final truth we must know the Revealer of truth. The nonChristian needs to first come to God through Christ; the Christian must pursue truth based on God's revelation in His Word and in His creation, assisted by the Holy Spirit. Otherwise we all search in vain.

Says Who?

When someone states a fact, we sometimes respond, "Says who?" This usually occurs when we doubt what they say. But what we are questioning is less the comment than the authority behind it—in other words, the source of the information.

All theologies, including our own, make statements of fact. But those assertions don't all carry the same authority. Theological statements originate in God's revelation, or human reasoning, or a combination of the two. We know which are more authoritative than others by how much their source is God rather than us. In his *Christian Theology* Millard Erickson proposes the following levels of authority for theological statements.[2]

First, direct statements of Scripture. These are most authoritative because they come directly from the Bible. An illustration might be, "God is love" (1 John 4:16). A simple assertion of fact—no human reasoning involved.

Second, direct implications of Scripture. These include the human step of a logical conclusion, so they carry a little less authority than the previous category.

Acts 12:21-23 directly implies that Herod was an arrogant man. The text does not say that but implies it very strongly.

Third, likely implications of Scripture. These are similar to the previous point but the conclusion is less obvious. The statement "most Thessalonian believers were converted from paganism, not Judaism," is likely true based on 1 Thessalonians 1:9. That text identifies them as converts from idol worship, which was unheard of among ancient Jews, but common among pagans.

Fourth, inductive conclusions from Scripture. These come from combining our interpretation of several passages. Galatians 4:14-15 can be taken to say the Galatians loved Paul so much they would have torn out their eyes to heal his sickness. Then, in 6:11, as Paul closes the letter, he mentions his large handwriting. By combining those passages, some conclude the following: "Paul had an eye problem or at least very bad eyesight." He may have, but the authority of that statement is diminished because it includes so much human reasoning.

Fifth, conclusions drawn from general revelation. General revelation, what we learn from God's creation, is less precise than special revelation, what we learn from His Word. General revelation must be clarified by special revelation. Consider this statement: "I sense the presence of Someone greater than I." Paul sheds light on that vague awareness in Romans 1:19-20 by affirming that God has revealed Himself in His creation, including human nature, thus we sense His presence.

Sixth, outright speculations. These are little more than personal opinions. They can be helpful but should be labeled as opinion. The statement, "Jesus is coming back in the year 2000" had little authority because it was speculation.

When anyone makes a theological statement consider the source. Is it from God, mankind, or some combination of the two? The answer helps us determine how believable the statement is.

Having Rights or Being Right

When you try to explain the Bible to a friend, you might get the response, "That's just your interpretation." That reply is most popular from those who disagree with another person's view, especially about the Bible. On the surface, it sounds innocent enough—we all have the right to our opinion. But having the right to our opinion is not the issue.

The level of thinking in our day has declined so much that people confuse the right to their opinion with the likelihood that their opinion is right. But those two concepts are unrelated. "But," your friend adds, "the Bible includes all those mysterious, contradictory statements. How can anyone think his view is better than any other view?" The question introduces many issues such as the understanding of statements, the role of logic, and the difference between a paradox and a contradiction. Let's consider those issues point by point.

First, God gave the Bible to be understood in common language by common people. Its meaning is not restricted to priests, church authorities, or any other elite group. Even though we may need scholars to help us grasp the Bible's hard parts, its meaning is usually quite clear if we approach it honestly.

Second, the Bible's understandability does not mean it can be interpreted any way we choose. We have no excuse for sloppy or lazy thinking to make it say whatever supports our preferences. Our interpretation of any statement is right only if it corresponds to the author's intent.

Third, our inability to understand everything in the Bible or in the universe does not mean that God, the source of both, is the author of confusion, or chaos, or irrationality. The fact that God's understanding exceeds logic does not mean it violates logic. He may at times be supra-rational, but He's never irrational. We don't pursue truth by avoiding logic.

Fourth, the Bible does include things beyond human understanding. But the presence of mysteries or paradoxes does not make the Bible incomprehensible, nor does it mean the Bible contains contradictions. A contradiction is a statement that says something can be what it is, and not be what it is, at the same time and in the same way. For instance, to say a shape is a circle and then say it is not a circle is a contradiction. The Bible never does that. The Bible does contain many examples of paradox, which is a statement that looks like a contradiction on the surface, but becomes more clear with more thought.

We are responsible to think clearly about what we can understand now, and trust God to explain more fully in eternity what we can't understand now. In the meantime, don't let your friend confuse you by merging two unrelated concepts—her right to an opinion and the likelihood that her opinion is right.

What's It All About?

During our times of deepest hurt or utter despair, we pause from the busyness of life and reflect on ultimate issues. We may ask, "What's it all about? What's the point of life? Why keep going?" The big picture that gives context to life is found in the Bible. Any short summary will skip a lot, but the general outline from the eternal past through human history into the eternal future looks like the following.

Before everything else, God lived in timeless perfection. Before the beginning of time and space, matter and energy, the One, infinite, living God existed. He was and is a Trinity—three centers of active personal consciousness relating to one another in complete, content, and joyous love.

The first recorded external act was creating everything from nothing. This marked the beginning of time and space, matter and energy, and all life other than His own. The first human pair were created unique—in the image of God. That means God placed within them some traits partially like His own. They also shared between themselves and with God a similar joy of relationship that God enjoyed within Himself.

But the first couple rebelled against their Creator, breaking the relationship between Him and them and between themselves. The universe was twisted out of its intended design. The image of God within the man and the woman was not destroyed but was disfigured almost beyond recognition.

Then, out of His mercy and love, God began the process of restoring the couple and their descendants. The only one who can fix something originating from God's hand is God Himself. So the second Person of the Trinity set aside the independent use and full display of His divine traits by becoming a man. Remaining equal with God and becoming equal with man, He could mediate between the two (Philippians 2:5-8).

The execution of the divine plan in human history began in Israel 2,000 years ago when the second Person of the Godhead came as Jesus. Some thirty-three years later He died to pay the penalty for sin required by God's righteousness and justice. What now lies between the human race and its Creator is no longer the sin, but Jesus Christ. So the issue for each of us now is, "Will you accept what Christ has done for you?" To reject His payment for one's sin is to remain alienated from God. To accept His payment for one's sin is to receive forgiveness and a new relationship with God—the status of God's child.

This new standing, however, is not the end of God's plan for us. Salvation is but the beginning. God aims to grow us into the likeness of His Son, Jesus Christ. God's plan for our restoration and transformation is comprehensive—what we are, what we know, what we do, integrated into a seamless whole. He plans to make us more than the original model, Adam; we're becoming like Jesus Christ. Even if we cannot see daily progress, we should be able to detect long-term movement in that direction. The goal of each Christian should be, "Am I more like Jesus now than I was in the past?" Whatever the details of our lives, that's what it's all about. That's the big picture.

God's Self-Disclosure

God's making Himself and His truth known to mankind is called "revelation." He reveals to us what we could not otherwise know. Revelation results from God's initiative, not from man's discovery. In other words, we don't find God; He reveals Himself to us. He is His own revealer; we are merely the recipients. God is the only source of knowledge of Himself.

God's revelation is necessary for us to know Him because we are so different from Him. In terms of capacity, God is infinite and we are finite. In terms of moral nature, He is holy and we are sinful. Because of those differences, God is inaccessible without His accommodating Himself to us by revealing Himself. We cannot know God or relate to Him unless He reveals Himself. God reveals Himself in two ways—general revelation and special revelation. These two kinds of revelation form a unity—each would be incomplete without the other.

God's general revelation is His communication to all people, at all times, in all places. It is general in two respects: (1) It is available to all people generally rather than to a select group; and (2) its content is general rather than specific. God's general revelation is found in creation, both in nature (Psalm 19:1-4; Romans 1:18-25) and in human beings created in God's image (Romans 2:14-16). Thus it appears to be more of this world than miraculous. The content of general revelation is only broad truths about God: He exists, He's powerful, and He's the Creator and Judge.

Because God is the standard of truth, His general revelation provides a basis for morality, a meaningful foundation for Christian witness, and a backdrop for the plan of salvation revealed in special revelation. But general revelation alone does not provide enough information to be saved, only enough to be without excuse for rejecting God. So we need more information from God— His special revelation.

God's special revelation is His communication to particular people at specific times and places, and is recorded in Scripture. It is special in two respects: (1) It is available selectively rather than universally; and (2) its content is precise rather than general. God's special revelation was given through unusual historical events like the Exodus, through divine speech as recorded in the Scriptures (Jeremiah 18:1; 1 Timothy 3:16), and in the incarnation of Jesus Christ (Hebrews 1:1-2), the most complete revelation of all. Thus it's more miraculous than natural. Special revelation expands and completes God's general revelation. This is especially true in that it tells us about God's plan of salvation through His Son Jesus Christ and how to live to please God.

Special revelation is needed to complete the partial truth of general revelation. With only general revelation, we would be accountable to God for rejecting Him, but ignorant of His provision for saving us. Christians should view God's currently available special revelation (the Bible) as our authority for truth and life. By studying it daily we know Him and how to live. The Christian response should be a consistent diet of God's truth in Scripture, to inform and guide us through life in this world.

God's Breath

When an author writes a great work, people call it inspired. Labeling Shakespeare's work inspired means it has a higher, more enduring quality than other writings. The biblical and theological meaning of inspiration is different; it means the writing is "God-breathed." This kind of inspiration surpasses human inspiration because it says the source of the material is God rather than man. Human inspiration is rare; divine inspiration is truly unique.

The apostle Paul writes in 2 Timothy 3:16 that all Scripture is inspired. He means the entire Bible and every word in it originates with God. This quality of being God-breathed includes the teaching expressed in the Bible and the very words of the Bible.

The inspiration process applied only to the original writings—what Moses, Matthew, Paul, and others personally wrote. The result applies also to accurate copies or translations of their autographs. The originals were perfect in every word, but copies or translations can include a few copying errors. Therefore, when theologians say the Bible is inerrant (without errors) they are speaking of the original text and accurate copies.

Inspiration does not mean that the prophets and apostles passively recorded what God audibly spoke. Inspiration is not mere dictation. Rather, the Holy Spirit guided the human authors so that, while preserving their different personalities and writing styles, they wrote without error the exact thoughts and words of God. This process is called the dual authorship of Scripture. The resulting textual precision was so detailed that Jesus said even the smallest letter and mark was correct (Matthew 5:18).

The practical conclusion of inspiration is that the Bible is our authority. Because it comes from God it carries God's authority just as a general's order carries the general's authority. And the Bible's authority exceeds the authority of any government demand, or social custom, or personal preference, even our own. What the Bible says, we must obey.

The two most obvious applications of this doctrine are learning and living what the Bible teaches. God gave His truth by this method so that His people would know and do what it says. This requires disciplined study, careful interpretation, and valid reasoning—a lifetime pursuit that is never completed, regardless of how much we eventually learn. The accumulation of Bible knowledge must be followed by applying that knowledge in life. As James writes, "Be doers of the Word, and not hearers only" (James 1:22, NKJV). Learning without doing mocks God's Word and deceives us. For God's children, learning and living God's inspired Bible should be as instinctive and routine as inhaling and exhaling.

To Err Is Human, Not Divine

If an English teacher writes an essay for her class, can they trust what it says? Not if it contains errors. Even the possibility of an error destroys the essay's reliability because they wouldn't know what to believe and what to reject. The same is true for the Bible. If it might include errors, we can't know what is true and what is false. The Bible's reliability is lost.

But God's writing of Scripture results in perfect accuracy. This view is called the doctrine of inerrancy. It means that the prophets' and the apostles' inspired, original writings included no errors. This doctrine does not mean that we understand the Bible completely or without difficulty, but that when all the facts are known, and it's correctly interpreted, it makes no mistakes.

Inerrancy and inspiration go together. A divine source and process demands that no errors result in the product. Inspiration refers to the divine source and process of writing Scripture; inerrancy refers to the product of that inspiration—a mistake-free Bible. Because inerrancy is the result of inspiration, it applies only to the Bible's original writing. Copies and translations do not possess inerrant status because God does not reinspire them.

Inerrancy is not limited to select subjects such as salvation or ethics but covers all the Bible's topics, including science and history. Recognizing that the Bible uses the common language and descriptions of the time of writing, no proven scientific or historical fact contradicts any accurately interpreted statement of Scripture.

But, one may ask, what difference does this doctrine make if we don't have the inerrant originals, but only copies and translations that might contain errors? On the surface, that sounds like a legitimate challenge. But through the efforts of textual criticism, the inerrant originals can be reconstructed to over 99 percent accuracy.

The simplest argument for this doctrine is the character of God. If He allowed errors into His Word, He is not the God of truth as the Bible claims in Titus 1:2 and Hebrews 6:18. Jesus said in John 10:35 that the Scriptures cannot be broken. He could assert Scripture's absolute authority only if He believed it was free of errors. So if the Bible is not inerrant, either Jesus was wrong or He lied.

The doctrine of inerrancy is so foundational that rejecting it has commonly led to abandoning other core Christian doctrines. Indeed, its denial by theologians, churches, or schools has often been the first step on the path to rejection of orthodox Christianity. Inerrancy, therefore, serves as the anchor of the Christian faith, and we dare not let it go.

God's Word Rules

Any statement is only as authoritative as the person making the statement. The boss's words carry more weight than the mail clerk's. The referee's decision over-rules the player's protest. It follows that if the sovereign Creator speaks, His words carry His ultimate authority.

This easily recognizable fact guides theology. A theological statement is accepted as true because someone with authority says it's true. That someone may be a person, an institution, or God. Because Christians believe that God is the final authority, His words are decisive regarding theological issues and all other issues.

Wayne Grudem equates the authority of Scripture with God's authority: "To disbelieve or disobey any word of Scripture is to disbelieve or disobey God."[3] This is the clear teaching of Scripture. The Bible claims such divine authority by describing itself as "God-breathed" (2 Timothy 3:16), harmonizing with Jesus' view of the Old Testament as "the word of God" (Mark 7:13), and with the prophets' repeated introductory statement, "Thus says the Lord."

The New Testament views itself as no less authoritative than the Old Testament. The apostles recognized their message as "the word of God" (1 Thessalonians 2:13). Peter conferred the same status on Paul's writings by classifying them with "the other Scriptures" (2 Peter 3:15-16). John labels his final book "the word of God and the testimony of Jesus Christ" (Revelation 1:1-2).

For the past thirty years, however, scriptural authority has been challenged in the Western world. Attacks have been leveled at specific authorities such as parents, teachers, and police, and at the very idea of authority as a concept. Accordingly, belief in the Bible is said to be culturally conditioned, and thus authoritative only if people choose to see it that way. In this view, society becomes the authority over the Bible. In reality, these people are not rejecting authority, but only relocating it from God to mankind.

The Bible's authority is one of the most practical Christian beliefs. If it is truly God's written Word, then to believe it is equal to believing God, and vice versa. Therefore, the Bible is the authoritative standard for all faith and life. The inescapable result of the Bible's authority is that we are to learn it, believe it, and obey it. Scripture should direct Christians' lives from individual choices to church decisions. Most churches would benefit from seriously and humbly comparing their own ministries to God's Word. Traditional but ineffective ministries, committees, and programs that are not found in Scripture should be candidates for termination if we truly believe that God's Word rules.

The Bible Is Exactly Enough

The Reformers' rallying cry was the Latin phrase, *sola scriptura*, "only Scripture." They meant that God had revealed in Scripture all He wanted us to know and do. It didn't need augmentation by popes or church councils. This doctrine is called the sufficiency of Scripture, meaning that the Bible contains everything we need for knowing God and living a godly life.

As the word "sufficiency" suggests, the Bible is enough, exactly enough. In 2 Timothy 3:15,17 Paul says Scripture "is able to make [us] wise for salvation" and it equips us "for every good work." In other words, knowing God and how to do what He expects is found in the Bible. The answers we seek about God, ethics, and life are in Scripture. So the Bible cannot be added to or improved upon by gurus, mystical experiences, pseudo-spiritual enlightenment, pop psychology, or even claims of direct insight from the Holy Spirit. God is not giving new revelation through other writings or church traditions or alleged visions. Nor are any of those equal to God's Word.

This doctrine prohibits us from adding to or taking from Scripture: "Do not add to what I command you and do not subtract from it, but keep the commands of the LORD your God that I give you" (Deuteronomy 4:2). It does not, however, limit God from writing more Scripture if He had so chosen. But Scripture's purpose of revealing God's plan of redemption is complete because the central events of that plan—Christ's death, burial, and resurrection—have occurred and been recorded.

This doctrine does not mean the Bible is exhaustive. God has not revealed everything He knows or all that we would like to know. But when the Bible does not address some issues of modern life, it guides us by broad principles. We must study, however, to find those answers; simply reading random passages provides little guidance.

We don't need to seek "truth" about God that's not in Scripture, or do things not in Scripture, or consider sin anything that Scripture does not call sin. According to Psalm 119:1, if we "walk according to the law of the LORD" we are "blameless," that is, without sin. Nor should we follow legalistic additions to Scripture. If it's not in the Bible, God didn't think we needed it. For instance, some Christians may think a church without a Wednesday evening prayer meeting has lost its spiritual passion. But the Bible's instructions about prayer do not require that we do it as a group at the church building at 7:00 P.M. on Wednesdays.

Finally, we should emphasize what Scripture emphasizes. Why place importance on things God doesn't? Did He miss the point of His own writing? Can we see more clearly than He does? Heresies and cults spring from such an imbalanced approach to Scripture, over-emphasizing obscure passages, and ignoring the Bible's clear teaching.

This doctrine is much needed today to counter the numerous false authorities competing with God's Word. This can be as true inside churches as outside. Perhaps the most pertinent but painful question churches should weigh is how much their human traditions or personal preferences, rather than God's Word, determine their decisions.

What's In and What's Out?

Why does our Bible include the sixty-six books it does? That question is addressed by the doctrine of the canon. "Canon" translates Greek and Hebrew words for a "measuring stick" or "rule" or "list." The theological meaning is a "standard" of authenticity. In common use, the "canon" of Scripture means the books that should be in the Bible because they're inspired by God.

The Old Testament: The thirty-nine Old Testament books were written between the fifteenth and fifth centuries B.C. The Jews believed that God stopped sending prophets about 435 B.C., so after that no one spoke or wrote words from God. The Jews apparently recognized those thirty-nine books by Jesus' time because none of their many theological disputes with Him raised any questions over which books were in their canon. Jesus and the New Testament quote Old Testament passages almost three hundred times, and every quote is from the thirty-nine books that have been handed down to us. Likewise, many of the five hundred Dead Sea Scrolls are commentaries, and they comment only on books in our canon.

The Apocrypha: These are Jewish books written between the last Old Testament prophet and the time of Christ. None were written by prophets, and they don't claim inspiration. The Jews never considered them from God, and Jesus and the New Testament never quote them. They weren't accepted by anyone until the sixteenth century when the Roman Catholic Church "canonized" them to counter the teachings of the Reformation. This introduces an important distinctive—Catholicism believes it grants authority to a book by its own decree. Protestants, like ancient Jews, believe that God's people merely recognize what is already authoritative because God wrote it.

The New Testament: Because Christ commissioned the apostles, they wrote with His authority. That apostolic authority was the main test to include a book in the New Testament canon. Early Christians considered the apostles' teachings equal to the Old Testament prophets' writings. In the late second century, Christians began listing books they considered authoritative. Two developments heightened the need to formally recognize God's Christian writings: (1) the rise of heretics who claimed new revelation from God; and (2) the Roman Empire's demand for Christians to surrender their sacred books to be burned. If the early Christians were going to die for

their Scriptures, they wanted to ensure it was for the right books. By the fourth century, Christian writings were being classified as "accepted," "disputed," "rejected," or "heretical." In 367 an Egyptian scholar named Athanasius specified the twenty-seven books of our New Testament, and thirty years later the Council of Carthage recognized the same list.

Why is God not writing more books? Because His most complete revelation has been given—His Son. God's revelation in Christ "in these last days" (Hebrews 1:1-2) implies that God is finished writing Scripture. Nothing can exceed what was given through Christ. Like the Jews, Christians believe that God gave and preserved His Word, and then led His people to recognize it. We can be confident that our Bible is what God wrote. Our response should be to learn it, let its truth form our minds and character, and obey it by applying its principles in life.

Do We Have a Corrupted Text?

THE BIBLE 15

Is our Bible true to the original text? Because the Bible was written centuries ago in Hebrew, Aramaic, and Greek, our English Bibles are translations of copies of prior copies. How do we know that the text we have has not been corrupted in this lengthy, complicated process?

None of the original Old Testament writings remain—they disappeared for two reasons. First, ancient Jerusalem was twice destroyed and the Jews deported. Those violent events made it nearly impossible to preserve written materials. Second, the Jews had such reverence for their Scriptures that when a copy began to wear out, they disposed of it with a ritual burial.

The lack of ancient copies would seem to hinder modern scholars' efforts to reconstruct the exact wording of the original. But the text we have is amazingly accurate because it was preserved over the centuries by the ancient scribes' meticulous copying rules. We can verify their accuracy by comparing copies of Old

Testament books found among the Dead Sea Scrolls, written between about 250 B.C. to A.D. 50, with the later Masoretic text, from which our Old Testament comes.

The scribes' procedure included the following: Nothing was written from memory, not even one letter. They counted the number of verses, words, and letters in each book, and then noted the middle verse, word, and letter of each. They kept detailed records to compare their counts to those of previous scribes. This demanding process almost guaranteed that any copying errors would surface which could then be corrected. Nothing was left to chance.

The issues surrounding New Testament transmission are different, but the resulting text is no less accurate. Like the Old Testament, no originals of the New Testament exist today. But we do have thousands of copies including fragments dating to a generation or two after the original. It is not out of the question to suggest that these earliest fragments may have been copied directly from the original.

Also at our disposal are the writings of the early church fathers who quoted so much of the New Testament that some scholars believe we could reconstruct it entirely if we lost all our copies. Such a wealth of documents, stored in the libraries of the world's great universities, gives textual experts a great advantage in reconstructing the exact wording of the originals.

As we might imagine when working with thousands of documents, we find variations in the copies. But the number of differences is exceedingly small—smaller than the variations among our English translations. Most are spelling differences, and none affects any significant doctrine. The result of such research is that we have no doubt about the exact wording of over 99 percent of the original New Testament.

What we have today, both Old and New Testaments, is what God wrote long ago. We can trust it, learn it, memorize it, and live it with confidence.

Turn on the Light

Before learning how we understand Scripture, we need to meet the third Person of the Trinity—the Holy Spirit. Just as we turn on a light to illuminate a room, the Holy Spirit's illuminating ministry turns on the light of understanding in the human soul. We should distinguish between three different but similar-sounding ministries of the Spirit: "Revelation" is the Spirit's giving Scripture; "Inspiration" is the Spirit's overseeing the human authors' writing of Scripture; "Illumination" is the Spirit's clarifying Scripture for the reader. We need this last ministry for three reasons: (1) God is so different from us that we can't understand Him without His help; (2) the Fall left all of us spiritually blind; and (3) sin hinders our spiritual receptivity.

This doctrine was neglected for centuries prior to the Reformation because the Roman Catholic Church taught that tradition, not the Spirit, was the key to interpreting the Bible. So, rather than relying on the Spirit for understanding the text, people merely accepted what the church said. But Martin Luther's teaching of the Bible resurrected the doctrine of illumination.

Jesus promised the Spirit as our ultimate teacher in John 14:26 and 16:13. The Spirit first overcomes our inborn spiritual blindness so that we might believe the gospel. We then grow spiritually as we are nourished by His Word (1 Peter 2:2-3) and as He enlightens us to the truth (1 Corinthians 2:12-13).

The Spirit's illumination is not automatic or universal. According to Paul, spiritual birth (regeneration), resulting in the Spirit's inner presence, is required because the person without the Spirit does not accept the things of God (1 Corinthians 2:14). Nor can we receive the Spirit's illumination if we persist in immaturity or a sinful life (1 Corinthians 3:1-3). We must also study (2 Timothy 2:15), applying sound principles of human interpretation. Illumination does *not* make study unnecessary; it makes study effective. It does not increase our mental ability, making us instant theologians, bypassing the normal process of logical thinking and common sense. Nor does it remove the need for human teachers (Romans 12:6-7) or imply that the Spirit violates or works without His written Word.

Illumination is not an emotional experience, heightened state of awareness, or ecstatic condition. It's the normal function of our relationship with the Spirit who always indwells the believer. It does not imply that we receive flashes of insight or unusual ability to discover special truths that others cannot find. Nor does it mean the Spirit gives new revelation, or guarantees the accuracy of our interpretations.

The Spirit's illumination is the linkage between God's recorded truth and the believer's rational mind. So we can pray, as Paul did, for the Spirit to work within us that we might understand and apply His Word (Ephesians 1:17-19). As we go to His text, we should pray for this insight from the original, divine Author. Prayerful, thoughtful, humble study of the Bible yields understanding as the Spirit uses our human efforts.

What Did He Mean?

Revelation, inspiration, and illumination are divine work, but interpretation is human work. God wrote Scripture to be understood by ordinary people, not just scholars, but at times we still misunderstand it. One reason is that the Bible is a collection of sixty-six writings in three languages, over fifteen centuries, by dozens of authors, in diverse styles, and for different audiences. Grasping God's meaning from such complex material requires "hermeneutics," taken from a Greek word that means "to explain or interpret."

We should approach God's Word honestly, letting it form our opinions rather than making it fit our opinions. Too often we search Scripture to bolster what we already think, rather than letting it teach us. But without a teachable spirit we're not learning the Bible, we're rewriting it. Because God's Word is authoritative, we cannot interpret it by our preferences or experiences; we must evaluate our preferences and experiences by using the Bible.

We should interpret the Bible as we interpret other material, according to the normal or literal sense. The

Bible does use figurative language, but the context usually signals its presence. We can learn to recognize the kinds of literature—poetry, parables, history—and different kinds of statements. A statement of historical fact is not the same as a command. For example, the fact that Jesus rode a donkey (Matthew 21:7) does not require us to ride donkeys instead of drive cars. So we must grasp the author's intended meaning for his initial readers before we can apply it to our world.

We also need to interpret within the context. History and culture form the external context, telling us about the world of the author and his audience. Biblical times were very different from ours, so we cannot make assumptions from ours to theirs. Why did the author write at all? What circumstances in his life or his audience's life prompted him to write? The internal context relates to the material immediately before and after the passage, as well as to the chapter, to the entire book, and to the whole Bible. Because Scripture best explains itself, studying the larger passage often answers questions about the smaller sections.

God's revelation is progressive through history, culminating in Jesus Christ's appearance in the gospels and the explanation in the rest of the New Testament. Therefore, later books often clarify earlier ones. As we compare the meaning of multiple books, we need to remember that the Bible is the product of one mind—God's. Because He is always truthful, His Word does not contradict itself. While a passage may have many applications, it has only one interpretation. We must know what God meant before we can apply it to life.

Sound interpretation benefits scholarly studies and personal devotions. It keeps us on track individually and prevents Bible study groups from merely swapping ignorance. God invested so much to give us His Word; we need to invest a little to understand what He meant. Our corporate response in our churches should be to emphasize ministries that teach Scripture, based on sound principles of interpretation, rather than on our own preferences or ideas or traditions.

Can We Know Him?

Mankind has always wanted to know God. But is that possible? He is very different from us—infinite, eternal, and self-sustaining—He is life itself. We are finite, temporal, and possess life only derived from Him. He is so different that we cannot know Him on our own—He exists outside our perceptions. But since we are created in His image, He is not "totally other" than us. By His self-revelation, we can know Him. His self-disclosure, however, introduces more questions: How much can we know about God? Can we be sure that what we think we know about Him is true? Where do we learn about Him?

18 GOD

These questions can be addressed only by God, because He is our only source of knowledge about Himself. Fortunately for us, He has revealed many things about Himself. Beyond His fingerprints in nature and within our own souls, He has revealed details through Jesus Christ (the living Word) and in the Bible (the written Word). Other evidence—outside God's revelation in Scripture—must be evaluated by Scripture.

How much can we know about God? We face a

dilemma because God is knowable in one sense, but unknowable in a different sense. That sounds like a contradiction, but it's not. Both sides of the statement about knowing God are true, but neither in an absolute sense. The distinction is between partial knowledge and complete knowledge. We can know something about God, but not everything.

Scripture teaches this mystery of not knowing and yet knowing God. Consider Job 11:7: "Can you fathom the mysteries of God? Can you probe the limits of the Almighty?" The clear implication is that we cannot know everything about God. But Jesus said in John 14:7, "If you really knew me, you would know my Father as well. From now on, you do know him." Jesus Christ reveals and explains who God is and what He is like. "Anyone who has seen me has seen the Father" (John 14:9). So Jesus taught that we can know God in part.

The current source of our knowledge of God is Scripture. Even though it does not record everything about Him, everything it does say is true. Through His revelation we can know that He is (Romans 1:20), who He is, His characteristics, His stated purposes, His usual providential acts through nature, and His extraordinary acts by miracles.

But the truth of God in the Bible, by itself, does not

guarantee that we possess this knowledge of God. That personal knowledge requires diligent study aided by the Spirit's illumination (1 Corinthians 2:13). One of the great joys of this doctrine is that we can spend all of life and eternity learning more about God. We can never learn all or too much about Him. We have already begun what may be our greatest eternal joy—coming to know the infinite, Holy One.

The Right Mix

We describe God with various traits called "attributes." Some of these are love, justice, and holiness. Theologians often list a dozen or more of these traits. Some readers mistakenly conclude that God is made of a number of different, unrelated ingredients like an enormous, invisible cake. As cosmic chefs we almost imagine that if we mix unlimited love and justice and holiness and other traits, we have deity.

Of course, it doesn't work that way. Not only could we not design and produce deity, but a mistaken notion within our theory derails the project. God's essence is not composed of multiple and diverse components. God is one simple essence that is accurately described by each and all of those attributes.

We might draw an analogy from chemistry. God is not comparable to a molecule made up of different atoms. He's one pure element without mixture of anything else. In other words, God is not some love over here, and some justice over there, and some holiness somewhere else. He's one simple, indivisible essence—

all of it accurately described as love, justice, holiness, and so on.

Another analogy might be drawn from a classroom marker board. When we say the board is white, flat, and hard we're not saying that it's white in one place, flat in another, and hard in yet another. The entire board is white, flat, and hard. Those traits do not compete or contradict one another. They each accurately describe the total board. So it is with God. He is all love, justice, holiness, and each of His other traits. Every attribute is equally true of all of God, and no attribute compromises or contradicts any other. This unified essence of deity is called the simplicity or unity of God. He is one, simple, pure, indivisible essence.

So, when we speak of one of God's attributes we should not think of it as a part of God separate from other parts. We are just emphasizing that particular trait for our purposes. Just as when we speak of the whiteness of the marker board, we're not suggesting the whiteness can be separated from the board's flatness or hardness. Likewise, when the Bible speaks of God's justice or love, it's not suggesting that God's other attributes are not involved—those other traits are just not being emphasized.

God's attributes are not something added to Him as though they were external to Himself. They are descriptions of God as He is, not traits He acquired or developed. All of His attributes are equally important, and none can be reduced if God is to remain God. His attributes don't increase or decrease in number or degree. An increase or decrease would indicate that God had become or had been less than perfect before or after that change. He is, was, and always will be one simple, perfect essence.

In our changing, temporary, and dangerous world, we have a source of strength, consistency, and provision— the living God. All His attributes, unified in a singular essence, remain on standby, ready to come to our aid.

To Be or Not to Be

We picture God's one, simple essence with descriptions that theologians organize into groups. These attributes are usually the same but theologians may label their groups differently, such as "attributes of greatness and goodness" or "moral and natural attributes" or "absolute and relative attributes." We will use a modified version of Millard Erickson's categories, listing God's attributes in five groups: attributes of being, infinity, moral purity, integrity, and love.[4] Here we will address God's attributes of being, including His spirituality, personality, and life. The other categories of God's attributes will appear in following sections.

When we say God is spirit we mean He is not physical substance. Jesus said, "God is spirit" (John 4:24)— He is immaterial and invisible. Nor is He a basic substance from which all other substance is derived— creation is not an extension of God Himself. Since He created all physical substance, He preexisted everything physical. As spirit, He's indestructible and immeasurable, unlimited by time or space. References to His "eyes" or "hands" are figurative language to help us comprehend God's actions that we associate with a physical body. For instance, by saying God has "eyes" we understand that God sees, but the Bible is not suggesting that God has eyes as we do.

God is also personal rather than impersonal. When Moses asked God His name in Exodus 3:14, God replied, "I am who I am." In that verse He proclaims His name and personal existence. Even the mere act of responding to the question reveals personality. He possesses personal traits such as self-consciousness, intellect, will, and self-determination. He thinks, feels, chooses, and enjoys relationships with other personal beings. God's personality is also revealed logically by man's personality, because the creature cannot have a higher trait than the Creator possesses. Since we have personality, He must also.

God is also alive, the very source of life, as Jesus said in John 5:26, "The Father has life in himself." Unlike the ancient gods of stone or wood, Jeremiah said God lives: "But the LORD is the true God; he is the living God, the eternal King" (Jeremiah 10:10). As the source of life, God did not derive His life from elsewhere. No other life source exists. He is it. He has always been alive as opposed to all other beings, who began life when He gave it to them. The continuation of His life does not depend on anything outside Himself because He is the eternal source of all life—the uncaused One. He doesn't even need to will His own existence—He simply is.

God is a living, personal spirit, the source of life, including our life, which He gave to us that we might relate to Him. We should thank Him for life and live every day for His glory and honor.

Bigger Than Big

Because God exceeds all limits, we say He is infinite. His infinite attributes describe His relation to space, time, knowledge, power, and change. Let's consider each.

God's unlimited relation to space is called "omnipresence." He is everywhere. First Kings 8:27 pictures this trait: "The heavens, even the highest heaven, cannot contain you." God is always everywhere, unlimited and unlimitable in terms of space. There is no place where He is not. Technically, as spirit, God is not spatial at all. He created space and is not contained within it. His infinity is not just bigger than all external space and smaller than any internal space—He is beyond all spatial measurements.

Because God's relation to time is unlimited, we call Him "eternal." Psalm 102:27 says His "years will never end." Psalm 90:2 states He is "from everlasting to everlasting." Time does not apply to Him—He is timeless. He was (and is now) before He created time, and He is simultaneously in the past, present, and future. He exists without end or interruption. But, since He is outside of time, seeing all events at once, He is aware of the succession of moments occurring in time.

God's unlimited relation to knowledge and wisdom is "omniscience." He knows everything and how to apply it. Psalm 147:4-5 declares, "His understanding has no limit." He knows all the facts about everything. He even knows every possibility from every contingency from an infinite number of sources. This includes all the details of the universe and us, and how to perfectly apply His knowledge to accomplish His plan.

God's unlimited relation to power is "omnipotence." He can do anything. The angel told Mary in Luke 1:37, "Nothing is impossible with God." He is able to fully execute His plan. He is in control of you and me — He is sovereign. But God's infinite power includes a built-in self-limitation. This inner restraint does not suggest inability in His power, but reveals that He always acts consistently with His nature. Thus He cannot sin, which would violate His holiness, righteousness, and justice. Nor can He do logically impossible things, such as make square circles, which is only a word game that says nothing about God's power.

The previous four traits are unchangeable. We call this God's "constancy." He does not and cannot change, develop, or diminish. Hebrews says of Him, "You remain

21

GOD

85

the same." God's constancy overlaps His being eternal. He cannot increase or decrease in any trait, which would imply previous or later imperfection, and thus less than deity. This trait does not mean God is immobile or inactive—He is dynamic, acting within His creation.

Since God is universally alive, there's no place or time He cannot be. Nor can He be taken by surprise. He is always and everywhere, accessible in our time of need, fully applying His infinite wisdom and power toward His plan and our good. Whatever our circumstances, we can always trust Him to be consistent and to do what's right. Whatever our challenges, problems, or fears, He knows and provides a solution fitting for our need. He is the ultimate and only fully trustworthy One.

Perfect Morality

Before meals kids might pray, "God is great; God is good. Let us thank Him for this food." That prayer may sound simple, especially coming from the mouths of children. But it contains solid doctrine. God is great—infinite, awesome magnificence; and He is good—ultimately pure and moral. His morality can be seen in three qualities: holiness, righteousness, and justice. Let's consider these three traits.

1. God directly asserts His holiness according to Peter's quote from Leviticus 11:44, "Be holy, because I am holy" (1 Peter 1:16). Holiness includes two sides: uniqueness and purity. Uniqueness means no one like God exists—He's completely distinct from everything else. Anyone else who claims deity is an imposter. Purity means God is unstained by anything less than perfection. Even though He knows and allows evil, He remains untainted by it. Both sides of His holiness should result in our reverence and worship.

2. God is also the standard of right and wrong, and He never deviates from it. We call this righteousness.

22

GOD

87

Abraham recognized this in Genesis 18:25 by asking an obvious question, "Will not the Judge of all the earth do right?" Righteousness also refers to the rightness of God's law: "The ordinances of the LORD are sure and altogether righteous" (Psalm 19:9). God applies this trait personally—His thoughts, words, and actions comply with His own standards. Applied in our direction, His righteousness gives us a basis for morality. Conforming to or deviating from God's character determines right and wrong for us. As a result our moral decisions can be based on something more reliable than mere personal preferences or the whims of the masses.

3. God requires His law to be obeyed, and He enforces it equally. We call this "justice." Peter admitted this in Acts 10:34, "I now realize how true it is that God does not show favoritism." Sin must be paid for, and good rewarded. We may not see the outcome of human events, either tragic or heroic, but eventually, in time or eternity, God will balance the scales of justice. Whether or not it's done when and how we like, His justice will satisfy His own requirements, and we're not to grow bitter or resentful at how He does it.

God's morality requires morality from us, and we can trust Him to judge fairly. We are to live righteously, treating others justly as He treats us, and He will hold us accountable to do so. God's children should accept His justice and treat others with justice. Contrary to the common view, life is not a series of neutral choices with no moral consequences. Every choice we make related to our thoughts, words, and actions reflects moral, immoral, or amoral standards, and God will judge based on His own character.

Who Can We Trust?

Across the spectrum of humanity, we feel lied to and manipulated. From the president to our friends, we don't know whom to trust. Truth is the urgent need of our time. But what is it and where can we find it? Even Pilate sarcastically asked Jesus, "What is truth?" (John 18:38).

Truth can be divided into three parts related to what we are, what we say, and what we do. Only God possesses all three perfectly, which we call His integrity. His being true is His genuineness or authenticity; His speaking the truth is called veracity; His proving to be true is His faithfulness.

First, God is genuine or authentic, "the true God" (Jeremiah 10:10) — not made from physical substance or human imagination. He is what He appears to be, and what He is supposed to be. He doesn't deceive us by misrepresenting Himself as something He's not. He is true and truthful, not because He conforms to something outside Himself, but because He's the very standard and definition of truth. We, His followers, should be genuine and consistent, not misrepresenting ourselves. To behave otherwise is to be hypocritical.

Second, God always speaks the truth and is therefore trustworthy. Everything He says is accurate to the way things are. Paul refers to God as the one "who does not lie" (Titus 1:2), meaning He does not and cannot lie, either deliberately or accidentally. All falsehood is contrary to His nature. His Word is fully trustworthy because it reflects His character. Because we represent Him, we're also to be fully honest in all we say and suggest. We are not to manipulate information to give a distorted view, but to speak simply, directly, and accurately.

Third, God proves to be true, reliable, faithful. He keeps His promises: "The one who calls you is faithful and he will do it" (1 Thessalonians 5:24). He never has to revise His Word because of a misstatement. The fulfillment of some promises may not come until eternity, but He keeps them all. Because He never breaks a promise, He does not make them lightly, not really meaning what He says. As His children, we should be known for the same—always keeping our word.

Wherever we search, we find perfect integrity only in God. Everything He says and does fits what He is. Because He exists and is truthful, He created His world to reflect truth. The Fall introduced distortion and falsehood, but truth still exists because He does. His people should love and pursue truth, and reflect it to others. Our lives should be, and can be, a mirror reflecting God's integrity. Those who know us should see our integrity in everything we are, say, and do, just as we see it in God whose image we bear.

True Love

Everyone loves love. The old saying, "Love makes the world go 'round" underscores its importance. But today "love" may mean nothing more than fuzzy feelings or aroused emotions or sexual desire. We discover authentic love only in the Trinity. The three divine persons have eternally, perfectly loved each other and us, described by four overlapping traits: grace, benevolence, mercy, and persistence.

Grace means God deals with us based on His character rather than our merit. He gives what we need rather than what we deserve. Paul writes in Ephesians 2:8-9, "It is by grace you have been saved, through faith—and this not from yourselves, it is the gift of God—not by works, so that no one can boast." We don't do good works to become God's children, but we will do good works as a result of being God's children. That includes treating others graciously. Many people see God's grace only in the grace we show them. We may be God's only advertisement in their lives.

Benevolence is God's unselfish concern for us. His

love takes the initiative, actively pursuing our benefit, rather than waiting to respond to something in us. Moses wrote of this in Deuteronomy 7:7-8, "The LORD did not set his affection on you and choose you because you were more numerous than other peoples . . . But . . . because the LORD loved you." He loves us for what He is rather than for what He can get. Because of God's benevolence toward us, we should love others the same way, actively seeking their benefit.

Mercy speaks of God's compassion toward the needy. Whereas grace responds to our guilt, mercy responds to our misery. God is gentle and kind to us, taking pity on our hopeless condition. "As a father has compassion on his children, so the LORD has compassion on those who fear him" (Psalm 103:13). Recipients of God's mercy should treat others mercifully, whether family, friends, or strangers. We are the most common channel through which God's mercy flows to the human race. Without our expression of His mercy, most will never see it in the course of their lives.

Persistence refers to God's patience. He continues to restrain His judgment and offer forgiveness, desiring that we turn to Him. "You, O Lord, are a compassionate and gracious God, slow to anger, abounding in love and faithfulness" (Psalm 86:15). Peter thought he was generous by suggesting we forgive others seven times. But Jesus said we should forgive not "seven times, but up to seventy times seven" (Matthew 18:22, NKJV). He didn't mean stop forgiving the 491st time, but keep forgiving regardless of the number. Our forgiveness needs to be waiting at the door of our hearts, to respond quickly and repeatedly to those who need it.

True love does not place ourselves at the center. It follows God's model, first by loving God, then by loving others as God loves them. With His love in us, we can love others to bless them rather than for what we might get in return.

What Do You Call Yourself?

Naming a baby today doesn't carry the same significance it did in the ancient world. Being named Tom rather than Jason, or Jessica instead of Kelly, says nothing about the kind of person that child is, or who the parents hope he or she will become. But in ancient cultures a person's name was more than identification; it represented the whole person, describing his nature. In a sense the name was that person, especially in the Old Testament. For instance, when Abraham "called upon the name of the LORD" (Genesis 21:33), he was calling upon God Himself. So when we read God's names in the Bible, God is telling us something about Himself.

The name *El* or *Elohim* is the generic word for "God," and occurs over 2,500 times in the Old Testament. The root word meant strength, power, or greatness. The plural *Elohim* indicates intensity or hints at the Trinity. The Bible often combines *El* with other names to describe God in more detail. *El Shaddai* characterizes God as the all-powerful, self-sufficient ruler. When Melchizedek blessed Abraham he referred to God as *El Elyon*, "the

God Most High" (Genesis 14:18-20). *El Olam* speaks of God's timelessness, often connected with the hope and security He gives believers: "Trust in the LORD forever, for the LORD, the LORD, is the Rock eternal" (Isaiah 26:4).

The most common Old Testament name for God, *Jahweh*, occurs about 6,800 times. It was the proper name for the God of Israel and never used for pagan gods. Scholars debate the exact meaning, but it probably comes from the verb "to be." In Exodus 3:14 when Moses asked God for His name so he could tell the Israelites who sent him, God replied, "I am who I am. This is what you are to say to the Israelites: 'I AM has sent me to you.'" Like *El*, *Jahweh* was combined with traits of God to form other names. The prophets frequently combined Jahweh with *Sabbaoth*, a military word for hosts or armies. The combination thus means the "Lord of hosts," probably referring to the angels, often translated "The LORD Almighty" (Isaiah 1:24).

In the New Testament, the Greek word *Theos*, translated simply "God," is the equivalent to *El*, appearing about 1,000 times. *Jahweh* is often translated *Kurios*, meaning "Lord," but also appears as a title for human lords and rulers. We find the most striking New Testament use of God's name in John 8:58-59. In a heated debate with the Pharisees, Jesus referred to

Himself as "I am." And the Jews who heard Him understood it as a claim to deity because "at this, they picked up stones to stone him," the punishment for blasphemy.

God's names mean something. They describe truly, though partially, what He's like. He is thus not an impersonal force or "mother nature" or a collective, universal consciousness. He is the infinite, powerful, yet personal One. His very act of revealing His names to us tells us that He desires a relationship with us. He wants us to know Him as well as about Him. Our lives demonstrate if we merely know information about this God, or if we personally know Him and interact with Him as we know and interact with others.

He's Here; He's There; He's Everywhere

How does God relate to the universe and to us? Is He distant and detached or nearby and accessible? The Bible teaches both. God is independent from the universe and removed from us, called transcendence; yet He is active in the universe and accessible to us, called immanence. He is both far and near, remote yet approachable.

Both sides must be held in balance. If we overemphasize either, the God of the Bible is lost. Excess immanence equates God with the universe—the God of pantheism (belief that the universe is actually God)—and His personality is lost. On the other hand, too much transcendence reduces God's contact with the universe—the God of deism (belief that God created the universe but then abandoned it)—and His involvement in the world, and with us, is lost.

God declares His immanence in Jeremiah 23:24, "Can anyone hide in secret places so that I cannot see him? . . . Do I not fill heaven and earth?" The obvious answer is that no one can hide from Him because He is everywhere and sees everything—He is immanent. New Testament believers are specifically said to be God's dwelling place. "Don't you know that . . . God's Spirit lives in you?" (1 Corinthians 3:16).

God's immanence implies that the universe is not a meaningless mass of fireballs interspersed with gigantic chunks of gravel. It is God's art, designed for our use and enjoyment. Because He has not abandoned it, we should neither abuse it nor let it rule us. We are to care for it but not worship it. We can also learn something of God by observing His universe. The systematic structure of what He made and still maintains says He is organized and logical rather than random and irrational.

God's transcendence means He is distant and different from us. "Who is like the LORD our God, the One who sits enthroned on high, who stoops down to look on the heavens and the earth?" (Psalm 113:5-6). God's transcendence is also moral—His holiness exceeds anything in us and everything we know. In Isaiah 6:3-5 the angels cry out, "Holy, holy, holy is the LORD Almighty." Isaiah responds, "Woe to me! . . . I am ruined! For I am a man of unclean lips . . . and my eyes have seen the King, the LORD Almighty."

God's transcendence means Someone higher than us exists. He establishes truth, controls history, and determines eternity. Our value is not set by ourselves but by Him who made us and rules over us. Even in eternity, we never become God. His salvation restores us to what He intended us to be; it does not make us what He is.

In Isaiah 57:15 God proclaims His balance between immanence and transcendence, "I live in a high and holy place, but also with him who is contrite and lowly in spirit." Finite humans and the infinite God never become one. He is always other than us, but always within our reach. Two practical consequences are His accessibility in our time of need and His worthiness of our worship. He is here, waiting to provide, and He is the awesome Ruler of the universe. We can praise Him for what He is as we receive His good gifts, as from a friend and a Father.

Three in One

The mystery of the Trinity has baffled people for centuries. But Scripture records ample evidence of the Trinity even though that word does not appear in the Bible. The doctrine may be difficult to understand but that does not make it untrue. Difficulty does not equal falsehood.

Let's consider several statements of definition. The Trinity is the Christian term for summarizing the biblical teaching about the oneness and diversity of the self-revealed God of the Bible. There is only one God, but within the unity of God exist three personalities consisting of the same divine essence. The one, true, living God is neither three gods nor three manifestations of one God. God is three centers of fully divine personal consciousness, each coequal and coeternal with the others, who together comprise one God.

The Old Testament emphasizes the unity of God to defend Israel against their neighbors' polytheism, the ancient belief in many gods. Deuteronomy 6:4 is the classic statement: "Hear, O Israel: The LORD our God, the

Lord is one." In contrast to the false gods of polytheism, the God of Abraham, Isaac, and Jacob is one and unique. Several Old Testament passages, however, suggest a complexity within God, such as Isaiah 6:8 where the Lord refers to Himself as both singular and plural: "Then I heard the voice of the Lord saying, 'Whom shall I send? And who will go for us?'"

The New Testament confirms the unity of God but introduces three personalities. Matthew 28:19 identifies the three, "Therefore go and make disciples of all nations, baptizing them in the name of the Father and of the Son and of the Holy Spirit." The three are distinguished, yet they bear one "name." These and other New Testament verses help explain the hints in the Old Testament passages.

The central idea of the Trinity is three-in-oneness, three personalities with one essence. Within the one God, three centers of personal identity and consciousness exist and relate to one another in perfect union. Each of the three is always equal and fully God, forever sharing the complete divine essence, none more or less God than the others. They are not three gods (tritheism), nor are they one person playing three roles (modalism).

The doctrine of the Trinity is critical for our salvation. Concerning Jesus, it's hard to imagine how a less-than-divine person could pay for our sins in a way that satisfies God's justice and righteousness. Regarding the Spirit, it's equally hard to imagine how anyone could give us spiritual birth and eternal life if He is less than God, the only author and source of life.

Since God is infinite and we are finite, we cannot fully understand the Trinity. But our limited understanding does not mean it's untrue. The Bible does not attempt to explain it completely, but it does teach it. Anything less than that Trinitarian understanding is less than the God of the Bible.

God's perfect harmony of internal relationships is the basis and model for the harmony we Christians should seek in our relationships. What a goal for every church—to love one another and be as united as the Persons of the Trinity, and then to send that love and unity into a world in desperate need.

He Did It His Way

Is history random or moving toward a destination? If it's the latter, what's behind it? Christians believe God has a plan and steers history toward His purposes. His ultimate goal is His own glory, and He'll achieve what He intends, even using mankind as His means.

The Bible says God's plan is eternal. Paul writes of God's "eternal purpose which he accomplished in Christ" (Ephesians 3:11). This means God's decisions are not made in response to events in time. They may be executed within human history, but they were determined in eternity. God does not surrender control of His universe. He does not let us initiate, forcing Him to respond. He is and always will be God; we are not and never will become God.

Because God is perfect and complete, His plan is free, uncoerced by internal need or external force. Isaiah 40:13-14 asks, "Who has understood the mind of the LORD, or instructed him as his counselor? Whom did the LORD consult to enlighten him, and who taught him the right way?" His plan includes everything and will be accomplished. God directly states, "As I have planned, so it will be, and as I have purposed, so it will stand" (Isaiah 14:24). He won't abdicate His throne to our demands.

What about the mystery of God's sovereignty and our will? God's rule is total. He wills what He wants and carries it out without fail. But our will makes real choices, and we're accountable for them. God has not revealed how He grants us free, responsible choice within His sovereign rule, but the Bible teaches that both sides of that mystery are real.

Like a theological chicken and egg question, the central issue concerns what is logically first: God's plan or man's choice. How one approaches the issue defines the difference between two theological systems known as Calvinism and Arminianism. Calvinists begin with God's plan. Man's decisions and actions are the consequence of it. God's plan is therefore not dependent on man. Arminians, on the other hand, place man's freedom at the center. God's decisions are a response to His knowing in advance what man will choose. God's plan is therefore a response to man's initiative.

A partial solution to this great paradox may be found in how we understand human freedom. Upon closer examination, we might discover that our will may not be as fully free as we usually think. But because we do make real choices, maybe we should call it "operational will" instead of "free will." Yes, I'm free to choose what I want, but I don't determine what it is that I want. Heredity, environment, and experience form my preferences long before I choose. If those earthly factors affect what I want, surely God can affect me even more. So, without hindering my ability to choose, God can influence my preferences, making it certain that I choose as He wills, while never violating my freedom. Paradoxical as it sounds, it's another part of the great mystery of God.

Because God's plan originates in eternity, He's never caught off guard in providing for us. He's neither surprised by the mess we make of our lives nor unprepared to meet our needs. He knew our problems and supplied solutions long before we or our problems existed. Furthermore, His plan can neither be derailed by human error or limitations, nor improved by human ingenuity or effort. He truly did it His way, and I can trust His plan for me.

First Things First

God is not passive, simply existing, doing nothing. He plans and then executes His plan. This raises a pivotal issue about how we interpret life, truth, and reality—where did everything come from, including us? The answer, according to the Bible, is God. "In the beginning God created the heavens and the earth" (Genesis 1:1). Early Christians considered this truth so important that it forms the first sentence of the Apostles' Creed: "I believe in God the Father, Almighty, Maker of heaven and earth." How did He do that, how is He related to His creation, and what does it mean for us?

The Bible says God made everything out of nothing. His mysterious process included no preexisting materials; He made those too. He truly started from scratch because He even made "the scratch." "The universe was formed at God's command, so that what is seen was not made out of what was visible" (Hebrews 11:3). As the verse says, His means of making the universe was simply His spoken word, the expression of His will.

Because He created everything, nothing came from

another source. Other than Himself nothing existed before He created. In a passage identifying Christ's role in creation, John writes, "Through him all things were made; without him nothing was made that has been made" (John 1:3). Paul agrees: "By him all things were created: things in heaven and on earth, visible and invisible, whether thrones or powers or rulers or authorities; all things were created by him and for him" (Colossians 1:16). According to that verse, His creative work included both spiritual and physical realms of the universe.

Before God created, there were no dimensions of height, width, or length, what we call "space," nor any succession of moments, what we call "time." Before creation, there was only God. And He created freely—creation is neither a necessary act of God, nor the result of external forces acting upon Him. He needs nothing and there were no other forces.

God's creation leads to several theological conclusions:

1. As the sole originating source of everything else, God is ultimate and sovereign. No cocreator exists.
2. The universe is not eternal—it had a beginning.
3. Nothing that is, either material or spiritual, exists apart from God.

4. The universe is not God Himself or an emanation of God. He did not create Himself or refashion any part of Himself as the universe.

5. Because God pronounced His creation "good" (Genesis 1:31), evil is not part of what He made. Created beings introduced evil by their rebellion against God.

6. Material reality is not less good or godly than the spiritual.

We should consider several practical conclusions that arise from God's creation. Each of these ideas can make a genuine difference in our lives:

1. Everything has value because God made it and gave it His stamp of approval.

2. Our artistic abilities reflect our being made in God's image, and thus their use glorifies Him.

3. Because creation by a designer implies order, scientific study of the universe is possible.

4. We are not eternal or self-sufficient, but exist to glorify God.

5. True worship begins with acknowledging God as Creator.

Who's the Boss?

When we see life's tragedies, we wonder "Why?" Even Christians ask how evil can coexist with an all-knowing, all-powerful, all-loving God. Is He the source of evil; the cause of sin? If not, where did sin and evil come from, and perhaps the most distressing question — why doesn't He stop them?

Those questions raise the topic of God's providence — His ongoing relationship to creation. God didn't make the universe, then abandon it; He stays in touch, preserving and guiding it toward His purposes. "In him all things hold together" (Colossians 1:17). "The Son . . . is sustaining all things by his powerful word" (Hebrews 1:3). None of creation is self-sufficient; everything depends on Him, including the processes of nature, the events of human history, and the circumstances of individual lives. His rule is hidden, but total.

So how can the sovereign King, who created and controls His world, allow evil within it? The problem is often stated as follows: If God is all-knowing, He's aware of evil; if He's all-powerful, He's able to stop it; if He's

30 GOD

111

all-loving, He wants to stop it. Therefore, because evil exists, God must *not* be one of those three things. So most efforts to resolve the question reject or reduce God's knowledge, power, or love, or deny the reality of evil. But none of those solutions work—God is all-knowing, powerful, and loving; yet evil really does exist.

The puzzle remains unsolvable in this life, but two factors help us comprehend it better. First, evil is the result of sin—decisions made by beings whom God created with choice. God decided to populate His universe with free beings rather than robots. For God to have prevented evil, He would have, and could have, made us different than we are. But, in His eternal plan, He knew it was better to create us as He did. We don't know why, but one reason may be to develop moral character within us, which requires freedom. That design allows the possibility of sin, but assures God more glory because He's more exalted by free beings with moral character than He is without them.

That brings up the second factor—eternity. This world's evil is not the end of the issue. The big ball game is not over, and we don't have the final score. Christianity believes that when time is swallowed by eternity, we'll understand better why God allowed evil. We may even partly grasp how God transforms evil into

His greater glory and our greater good.

The universe and all within it, including us, follow God's blueprint. We're not left to the fate of impersonal forces. God remains concerned and active in human affairs. All the events in our lives are opportunities for us to trust Him. Much mystery remains, but we trust that in His love, wisdom, and power, He will do what's right.

The Cosmic Thug

Comedian Flip Wilson is famous for his line, "The Devil made me do it." That easy excuse reveals the common cartoon view of Satan. But he's no joke. Satan is a personal, spirit being whose name means "adversary or accuser." Despite being known as "the Devil" he's a beautiful, angelic creature with abilities exceeded, apparently, only by God (Ezekiel 28:12-15).

Scripture calls him by many names that depict what he's like and what he does: tempter (Matthew 4:3), enemy (Matthew 13:39), murderer (John 8:44), father of lies (John 8:44), the prince of this world (John 12:31), the god of this age (2 Corinthians 4:4), the ruler of the kingdom of the air (Ephesians 2:2), the evil one (1 John 2:13), the great dragon (Revelation 12:9), the ancient serpent (Revelation 20:2). The list exposes his grizzly résumé of evil.

As part of creation, which God pronounced good (Genesis 1:31), Satan was not originally evil. But by Genesis 3 we find him in the garden tempting Eve to sin. Some theologians think Isaiah 14:12-14 and Ezekiel

28:12-15 refer, at least in part, to Satan's fall. Others believe those passages are only about the kings of Babylon and Tyre respectively, but both accounts exceed what could be true of any earthly ruler. If Satan is the prophets' subject, his rebellion is described in his own words: "I will ascend to heaven; I will raise my throne above the stars of God. . . . I will make myself like the Most High" (Isaiah 14:13-14).

Satan tried to destroy Jesus by killing Him as a baby (Matthew 2:16) and by tempting Him as a man (Matthew 4:1-11). Christ, of course, survived both attacks and secured Satan's defeat at the cross (Colossians 2:15). But God allows the evil one to wreak havoc on the human race prior to the execution of his sentence. Satan now rules the unbelieving world system (2 Corinthians 4:4; Ephesians 2:2) known as "the dominion of darkness" (Colossians 1:13). He also opposes believers with fierce hatred (1 Peter 5:8) even while masquerading "as an angel of light" (2 Corinthians 11:14). Likewise, "his servants masquerade as servants of righteousness" (2 Corinthians 11:15) as he schemes to deceive us by another gospel (2 Corinthians 2:11; 11:3).

But he will not win. His doom was pronounced immediately after he caused our fall (Genesis 3:15). Paul looks forward to the culmination of Satan's judgment in

Romans 16:20, "The God of peace will soon crush Satan under your feet." Satan and his demons will eventually be cast forever into the lake of fire (Matthew 25:41; Revelation 20:10).

Despite his power and ferocity he's a finite creature (neither omnipresent nor omnipotent), and "the one who is in [us] is greater than the one who is in the world" (1 John 4:4). "The reason the Son of God appeared was to destroy the devil's work" (1 John 3:8), and He succeeded. We are well equipped to resist as we "put on the full armor of God so that [we] can take [our] stand against the devil's schemes" (Ephesians 6:11). Paul reminds us that "the Lord is faithful, and he will strengthen and protect [us] from the evil one" (2 Thessalonians 3:3). Christ has defeated him, and we share the victory.

God's Messengers

Our materialistic culture resists belief in God but loves angels. From gift shops to book topics to TV shows, angels are riding a wave of renewed favor. They're not the subject of theological speculation as in the Middle Ages, but the trendy rage of marketers cashing in on a surge of popularity. Some people almost worship angels and everything about them.

Angels are not dead humans, or friendly humanoid creatures who help us out of life's jams as depicted on TV. They are personal, immortal, spirit beings created with intelligence and powers beyond ours. God made them early in His creative scheme since they celebrated when He laid the earth's foundation (Job 38:4-7). The Bible calls them by many names: "sons of God" (Job 1:6, NKJV), "holy ones" (Psalm 89:5), "watchers" (Daniel 4:17, NKJV), "heavenly host" (Luke 2:13), "thrones, powers, rulers, authorities" (Colossians 1:16), and "spirits" (Hebrews 1:14). Many kinds of angels may exist, but three identified classes are cherubim (Psalm 80:1), seraphs (Isaiah 6:2), and the four "living creatures" of Revelation 4:7-8.

32 | GOD

117

Angels possess will and intelligence (2 Samuel 14:20) although not omniscience (Matthew 24:36). As "mighty ones who do [God's] bidding" (Psalm 103:20) they have great but limited power. They praise God (Psalm 148:2) and administer His affairs on earth (Daniel 12:1). They observe our lives (1 Corinthians 4:9) and protect us (Psalm 91:11). They communicate God's message (Acts 8:26) and sometimes execute His judgment (Acts 12:23). They announced God's reconciling ministry, especially during the early years of the church (Acts 10:3). They will join Christ when He returns in triumph (Matthew 25:31).

The Bible identifies only two angels by name. Michael seems to be Israel's special protector and leader of the other angels (Daniel 10:13,21; 12:1; Jude 9; Revelation 12:7). He holds the title "archangel" (Jude 9), suggesting an angelic rank structure. Gabriel speaks as heaven's special envoy, communicating important messages for God (Daniel 8:16; 9:21; Luke 1:19,26-28).

Some Old Testament passages speak of "the angel of the Lord" in a way that sounds as if God Himself, perhaps the preincarnate Son, is appearing to humans. "There the angel of the LORD appeared to [Moses] in flames of fire from within a bush. . . . Then he said, 'I am the God of your father, the God of Abraham, the God of Isaac and the God of Jacob.' At this, Moses hid his face, because he was afraid to look at God" (Exodus 3:2,6). Similar incidents occur in Genesis 16:7-13; 22:11-12; 31:11-13; and Judges 13:21-22.

The angels' obedience provides a positive example for us. They also watch us, applauding our faithfulness and mourning our sin, while always ready to come to our aid. We should be cautious about claims of information delivered by angels because Satan masterfully counterfeits the real thing. Alleged angelic messages that are inconsistent with God's Word are not from God's messengers—they never violate His message.

Angels are mysterious, fascinating creatures, but not to be prayed to, chased after, or worshiped (Colossians 2:18). They are higher than we are now, but we will be higher in eternity. Paul says we will even judge angels (1 Corinthians 6:3). We can look forward to the day when angels and humans will praise God together.

Satan's Henchmen

The 1970s movie *The Exorcist* terrified millions with its grizzly portrayal of demon possession. Audiences exited theaters wondering, "Are demons real?" and "Can they actually do that?" Like most Hollywood renditions of almost any theme, a little truth mixed with a lot of sensationalism sells tickets, and *The Exorcist* hit the jackpot.

The Bible says much about demons but offers few details of their origin. They are supernatural, personal, spirit beings, created with will and intelligence. They possess superhuman strength and knowledge including the appearance of telling the future (Acts 16:16). God created them good as angels, but they evidently fell by joining Lucifer's rebellion against God. His title "prince of demons" (Matthew 12:24) implies that they are his spiritual underlings. That cosmic conflict still rages between the kingdom of Satan (the prince of this world), and the kingdom of God (the Creator of the universe).

We don't know how many demons there are, but some theologians conclude from Revelation 12:3-4 that one-third of the angels joined the spiritual mutiny. The

GOD | **33**

120

wording of Ephesians 6:12 suggests a rank structure among demons consistent with the levels of authority among angels in Colossians 1:16. If demons are fallen angels, we would expect that parallel rank structure.

As Satan's emissaries, demons execute his game plan. In their war against God they attack, tempt, and accuse His people. They may cause mental and physical illness (Luke 13:11), but they specialize in hindering our spiritual progress (Ephesians 6:12). They even influence entire nations and their rulers (Daniel 10:12-13). With their supernatural awareness of God, they know the truth, but twist it for their purposes (James 2:19). They promote false religion even within the church (1 Corinthians 10:20-21). The Bible warns that demonic activity will increase during the end times (1 Timothy 4:1).

Most New Testament references to demons are connected with their possession of humans. Jesus encountered many such cases and, sometimes after a dialogue with the demons, cast them out by a simple command (Matthew 8:29-32). While unbelievers may be subjected to this dreadful condition, Christians are not. Belonging to Christ, indwelt and sealed by the Holy Spirit, protects God's children. Demon possession can occur today in unbelievers, but spotting a demon in every person with an illness or problem is unwarranted.

Compared to us, demons have extraordinary power, but compared to God, they are very limited. Christ has already won the final victory over them, and their doom is certain—eternity in the lake of fire (Matthew 25:41; Revelation 20:10). God has provided our battle equipment for our role in the mopping-up operation (Ephesians 6:10-17). In the meantime, we should avoid two extremes: dismissing the reality of demons on the one hand, and being too intrigued by them on the other. We need not fear, but can trust Him who won our victory.

Where Did We Come From?

The subject of human origins remains one of the most hotly debated issues of our time. It affects more than our views on religion; it determines our thinking in almost every field: science, politics, economics, law, education, and ethics. So what is our origin? Where did we come from and why? Most people answer in one of two general ways: a random accident from nature's impersonal forces (evolution), or the deliberate, designed act of a personal intelligence (creation by God).

But a variety of views exists even among those who believe God was involved. Those who believe our beginning was from God choose from four views:

1. Immediate creation—God created everything in its final form in six literal twenty-four-hour days without using preexisting materials. He directly and supernaturally created Adam and Eve.

2. Deistic evolution—God created matter, energy, and natural laws which control and develop that matter and energy. But He then ceased His activity, leaving evolutionary processes to act on their own. His involvement

34 MAN

in our origin is only that initial, indirect creation of the matter, energy, and universal laws.

3. Theistic evolution—This view is similar to deistic evolution but God maintains a more active role in the evolutionary process. He created a spiritual nature and implanted it within one of the highly evolved primates, and called it "Adam."

4. Progressive creation—God initially created out of nothing much of His creation, but in a series of stages, over a long period of time, He created more out of nothing. This view is similar to immediate creation except that natural changes may occur within a species, and it allows more time than seven literal days. In this view God directly and supernaturally created Adam and Eve just as He did in immediate creation.

Because God is all-wise and all-powerful, independent, and self-sufficient, He did not *need* to create anything, including mankind. Why, then, did He create? We should exercise caution when trying to evaluate God's motives, but theologians may be right when they answer that it simply pleased God to create. A creation, especially a race of beings like mankind, reflecting His image, would apparently give God greater glory and joy than He would otherwise have.

One challenge of the origins issue is whether or not

we fulfill our purpose for being. Do we choose to glorify God or ourselves? If we choose ourselves, we're idolaters, unintentional perhaps, but idolaters nevertheless.

Mankind is unique among God's creation. Genesis 2:7 says, "[God] breathed into [Adam's] nostrils the breath of life, and the man became a living being." Nothing else in God's creation, not even the angels, receives this special, direct implanting of life from God. Because we alone possess this direct God-given nature, we are distinct from the rest of creation and have intrinsic value. Nothing in this world, neither human achievement nor self-esteem, can give us greater value than being created directly by God. Our searching, our possessions, our accomplishments cannot improve upon our origin at the hands of our Creator. We are the Master's masterpiece designed to praise Him as only we can.

A Lot Like God

Deep within our souls we search for a sense of identity. Built into each of us is a desire to know who we are, often expressed as "finding oneself." As a child we identify with our parents. As a young teen we often identify with our peers. As young adults we begin to wonder in a more serious way who we can identify with. To whom can we trust our lives and our souls?

Christians find the answer in the Bible's first two chapters—we can identify with God because we're created by Him. We are different from everything else God created because we're made in His image and likeness. "Then God said, 'Let us make man in our image, in our likeness, and let them rule over the fish of the sea and the birds of the air, over the livestock, over all the earth, and over all the creatures that move along the ground.' So God created man in his own image, in the image of God he created him; male and female he created them" (Genesis 1:26-27).

Being created in God's image and likeness is not said of anything else in the universe, not even the angels.

MAN | **35**

Theologians debate the exact meaning of the image and likeness of God, but it means we are in some way like God, possessing and displaying some of His traits. God used Himself as the pattern for creating us. Of everything in the created universe, we are the most like God. We are the pinnacle, the masterpiece of His creative art.

Most theologians believe the image of God is a combination of features rather than a single trait. Since these features are true of God's image, they also describe God. The image is found in our spiritual essence, our personality with self-awareness, a mind, and a will, and our moral accountability. As Genesis 1 indicates, we also exercise dominion or authority over the rest of God's creation as the result of possessing the image of the sovereign God.

But God's image in us is not now what it was at creation. It is damaged and distorted by the Fall; but it's not destroyed. The Fall resulted in mankind being totally depraved (Genesis 3:1-19; Romans 3:23). This does not mean we are as evil as we can possibly be, but every aspect of our being is affected by the Fall. Sin has damaged every part of the human being including God's image.

However, God is reversing the damage. Part of His redemptive purpose and process is to renew His image in mankind to its original reflection. After salvation we grow spiritually, becoming more like Christ. Because Christ is God, He is exactly like God. As we become more like Him, God is restoring His image in us to His initial intent.

God designed and manufactured the human race so that He might enjoy a personal relationship with us. Mankind's destiny, therefore, centers around the issue of possessing or not possessing a relationship with the Creator. We never know who we are until we are related to that One who made us in His own image. When we know Him we can know ourselves. We can then live as He intended, and enjoy Him and the good things He made.

What Are We Made of?

Theologians debate if humans are three parts (body, soul, and spirit), or two (body and soul/spirit as one entity). The view that we're made of three parts is known as trichotomy. It believes that our *body, soul,* and *spirit* relate to the physical world, other created beings, and God respectively. Trichotomists appeal to 1 Thessalonians 5:23, "May your whole spirit, soul and body be kept blameless at the coming of our Lord Jesus Christ" and Hebrews 4:12, "For the word of God is living and active. Sharper than any double-edged sword, it penetrates even to dividing soul and spirit. . . ." But trichotomists do not identify a difference between the essences of soul and spirit. They speak of capacities to interact in different relationships; one toward creatures, one toward God.

The two-part view of our nature is called dichotomy. We contact the physical world through our material body, and we relate to other living beings through our immaterial soul/spirit. Historically, most Christians have held this belief, contending that "soul" and "spirit" are interchangeable terms for our immaterial essence, not two

36 MAN

129

different parts of our being. Mary's parallel statements in Luke 1:46-47 illustrate this interchangeable use: "My soul glorifies the Lord and my spirit rejoices in God my Savior." John also appears to use the words synonymously when describing Jesus' *soul* as troubled in John 12:27 (NKJV) and then Jesus' *spirit* as troubled in 13:21.

A less common opinion among Christians is monism, the notion that we're an indivisible unity. Monists believe body, soul, and spirit all refer to our "self" or "life." Monism is hard to mesh with Scripture, however, because it disallows any conscious existence between physical death and resurrection. But Jesus revealed His belief in that intermediate state by telling the thief on the cross, "Today you will be with me in Paradise" (Luke 23:43). And Paul says, "To be away from the body [is to be] at home with the Lord" (2 Corinthians 5:8).

Since trichotomy and dichotomy both claim biblical support, how do we reconcile them? One solution is that both are true—a dichotomy of substances and a trichotomy of functions. Our essence is made of two components, material and immaterial, functioning in three relationships: our body to the physical world, our soul to other creatures, and our spirit to God.

How does God give each person a soul/spirit? Does He directly implant a newly created one in each person, called creationism (not to be confused with the creation/evolution issue), or is the soul/spirit passed down through the parents' genes, called traducianism? The Bible says little on the subject, but a problem arises with creationism. Because every person is born with a sinful nature (Ephesians 2:3), creationism suggests that God created sinful human souls, which contradicts God's holiness. Therefore, traducianism seems more likely.

Some details of our own makeup are not revealed to us. God didn't think it essential that we have answers to those questions. What is essential and revealed is that God made us with an immortal nature and capacity to know and relate to Him forever. In eternity, we'll understand more of the questions that now baffle us. In the meantime, we can know, love, and enjoy our Maker while we ponder His mysteries.

Our Utility Infielder

A utility infielder's value to his baseball team comes from his many abilities. He can do whatever is needed—play first, second, third, or shortstop. In a similar way, our soul possesses multiple skills—thinking, feeling, choosing, and distinguishing right from wrong. These functions blend into a unity sometimes called our "heart," the center of our immaterial self. We label these overlapping components mind, emotions, will, and conscience.

Our mind is our ability to perceive, understand, reason, and store information. Because the human mind is finite it cannot know everything, but as a reflection of God's mind it can know truly. God revealed and recorded His truth in statements understandable by the human mind (Luke 24:45). Both the Holy Spirit and our sinful nature influence our minds, swaying us toward or away from God (Romans 8:6-8). The Spirit transforms our lives by the Word our minds learn (Romans 12:2; Ephesians 4:23), thus developing "the mind of Christ" in us (1 Corinthians 2:16).

Our emotions represent our capacity to feel good or

MAN | **37**

bad toward events and people. Our emotions don't contain information as our mind does but merely respond to other influences. They work best when the mind controls them rather than when they rule the mind. Renewing our mind develops the fruit of the Spirit including (emotional) self-control (Romans 12:2; Galatians 5:23). So the foundation of life is not how we feel but what we think. Our emotions cannot be fully satisfied by people or anything in this world, but only by God who made us for Himself.

Our will is our faculty of choice. We may speak of "free will" but our fallen will is not truly free, although it still works. Only Adam and Eve enjoyed truly free will, but their choosing against God forever restricted their future options, and ours. Because our will is now tainted, in bondage to its own sinful tendencies, it cannot consistently choose what is good (Romans 7:18-19). We still select what we want, but our desires are corrupted by the Fall as well as influenced by factors beyond our control. Only God's grace through salvation and spiritual growth restores freedom to our will, which can increasingly choose for God and the good.

Our conscience gives us our capacity to distinguish between right and wrong, and also prods us toward good decisions and actions. Adam and Eve's hiding from God after their sin displays the result of a working conscience (Genesis 3:8-10). But if the conscience is damaged, it stops working and grows insensitive and unresponsive (1 Timothy 4:2). On the other hand, by learning and using God's Word, we develop our moral sensibility (Hebrews 5:14).

God's revealed truth in the Bible sustains the process of life. Paul explains the means of a changed life in terms of the role of the mind: "Do not conform any longer to the pattern of this world, but be transformed by the renewing of your mind" (Romans 12:2). When God's Word saturates our mind, our emotions respond to His truth and all that is good; our will consistently makes right decisions; and our conscience alerts us to danger while approving what is right. Consistent intake of God's Word, our spiritual nourishment, leads to transformation.

More Valuable Than Money

If I wasted a $10 million gift from God, you'd call that irresponsible. But we each possess a more valuable gift than money—a rational mind, our ability to perceive, understand, reason, and store information. Our mind is an indispensable part of God's image and the means by which we grow in the knowledge of God (Colossians 3:10).

But the Fall damaged the human mind, rendering us unable to recognize and accept God's truth. After spiritual birth, however, the Spirit illumines our minds, enabling us to grasp and respond to His Word. Such divine aid doesn't remove our need of study because the Spirit won't zap us with supernatural theological insights. He uses instead the fruit of our study to grow our souls.

38 MAN

Under the Spirit's guidance, faith and reason work together. Faith opens the door for the Spirit to enlighten our reason so that we recognize and accept His truth. Once reborn, we're in God's restoration process, becoming more like His Son, the *logos*, "the word, thinking, rationality" of God. Jesus prohibited unthinking spirituality by commanding us to love God with our *mind* (Matthew 22:37), and Paul ordered our transformation by "the renewing of [our] mind" (Romans 12:2).

Our model of rational thought is the *logos* Himself, the thinking God, who became one of us. We know from Luke's story about twelve-year-old Jesus accidentally being left in Jerusalem that He had studied His Hebrew Bible. We find Him at the temple discussing theology with the rabbis who were astounded at His knowledge (Luke 2:42-47). And these were the big-brain rabbis from the intellectual center of Judaism. Jesus, our example, had developed and used His mind because He knew He was responsible to His Father to do so. By thinking and thinking well, we reflect the *logos*, and bring glory to God.

Our Christian forebears respected the mind. Seventeenth century Puritan pastor Cotton Mather said, "Ignorance is not the mother of devotion, but of heresy." Over the next two centuries, however, the anti-intellectual tone of the revivalist movement replaced Puritan thinking. Early in the twentieth century, Christians largely rejected J. Gresham Machen's warning not to retreat from the coming war over ideas, and they withdrew from the broader intellectual culture. In 1980, Charles Malik warned that the church's greatest danger is anti-intellectualism—the rejection of using our mind in the service of Christ. More recently the warning was sounded again by J. P. Moreland in his book *Love Your God with All Your Mind*.[5]

The future of the American church rests in large part on our response to the repeated warnings of these insightful brothers. If we intend to influence our culture for the kingdom of God, we must resubmit our mind to the discipline of rigorous, rational thought. Daily, serious study and meditation on the Bible, theology, apologetics, and church history will reward our efforts individually and as a church.

The Internal Judge

A judge identifies and condemns violations of the law. The human conscience does the same in the soul, "distinguish[ing] good from evil" (Hebrews 5:14). Our conscience is our inner warning system, detecting violations of internal standards and pronouncing us guilty. Even unbelievers without the Word "show that the requirements of the law are written on their hearts, their consciences also bearing witness, and their thoughts now accusing, now even defending them" (Romans 2:14-15). Paul was telling Jews that even Gentiles, who did not have the written Scriptures, possessed an internal sense of right and wrong.

MAN | **39**

People in all societies possess conscience. Their specific system of right and wrong may vary from one culture to another, but they all exhibit moral notions of some kind. God designed us with moral judgment as part of His image. "The lamp of the LORD searches the spirit of a man; it searches out his inmost being" (Proverbs 20:27). Conscience is standard human equipment.

The Fall distorted that inner sense of right and wrong, but even in our fallen state our conscience retains some awareness of God and His ideals. Most people, including unbelievers, recognize evil when they see it. Paul says even the vilest people "know God's righteous decree that those who do such things deserve death" (Romans 1:32).

Our conscience is pliable, influenced for good or bad by what it's fed: parental training in God's Word (Deuteronomy 6:6-7), education and society, personal habits and customs. Because our conscience can embrace wrong principles, developing away from God, it's not always a reliable guide. If we suppress our conscience, ignore its promptings, and continue to sin, we find it easier to violate our conscience in the future. Eventually, even the grossest sins don't disturb us. In extreme cases the conscience grows so calloused that it's virtually impenetrable, rendered completely numb to thoughts of right and wrong (1 Timothy 4:2).

The Spirit informs our conscience through our learning His Word. The spiritual growth process then reforms our thinking, speaking, and acting to fit God's intent. We can mature so that we keep a clear conscience before God (1 Peter 3:16; Acts 24:16), "able to test and approve what God's will is—his good, pleasing and perfect will" (Romans 12:2).

Society's best hope is learning and applying God's truth so that our conscience reflects His justice and mercy for everyone. Throughout history, wherever the Bible influences culture, human conscience echoes God's design for humanity, improving the quality of life for all. Government functions best when enacting and enforcing laws consistent with Scripture, protecting citizens from evil (Romans 13:1-5). Only a return to God's Word by individual Christians and within churches, resensitizing our conscience, will reverse the current trends toward violence, cruelty, and inhumanity.

As simplistic as it may sound, the most significant impact you and I and our churches can have on our world may be learning God's standards so that our consciences conform to His will, and then living accordingly in society. The effect of living His kingdom principles in real life relationships may alter this world's evils more than any politics or preaching.

The Marred Masterpiece

God created mankind morally pure and in His own image to be His coregent over this world, enjoying communion with Himself. Adam and Eve were authorized to enjoy the production of Eden (Genesis 3:2), banned only from eating from the tree of knowledge of good and evil (Genesis 3:3).

Sin predates the Garden of Eden, as a result of Satan's revolt against God (Isaiah 14:12-14). That cosmic conflict forms the background for the fall of the human race, the turning point of moral history. Satan guided sin into the garden through the serpent's tempting Eve to eat the forbidden fruit. His challenge was an attack on the veracity of God's Word and the validity of God's authority.

Eve succumbed, and Adam, the head of the race, followed. Underlying the seditious act was unbelief—doubting God and believing the tempter. The central issue was who would be God—God or us? God's masterpiece, the first human pair, now stood condemned before their Creator, their moral innocence shattered.

40 MAN

Mankind's inner disposition changed from obedience to rebellion, God's jurisdiction and wisdom replaced by self-determination and pride.

God had warned of the outcome—death (Genesis 3:3). Spiritual death arrived immediately, breaking their intimate relationship with God, pictured in their expulsion from the garden, then physical death, experienced first by their son Abel (Genesis 4:8), later by Adam and Eve. But the Fall's effects spread beyond the first family to all the human race. The image of God in all was disfigured, although not lost. Sin was credited to every descendent of Adam; death awaits us all; and we inherit a sinful drift. God's created world was cursed, resulting in man's labor to live (Genesis 3:17-19) and woman's pain of labor to perpetuate life (Genesis 3:16). But in the midst of catastrophe God first announced the promise of redemption (Genesis 3:15).

Is the story history or mythology? The Bible portrays it as a true event. The genealogies of Genesis 5, 10, and 11 picture Adam as much as Abraham, Isaac, and Jacob in space-time history. Paul wrote of Adam, Moses, and Christ in parallel, historical fashion (Romans 5:12-19; 1 Corinthians 15:22). Wherever the Bible speaks of the Fall or its consequences, it bears the mark of history.

The Fall answers our most sobering questions. Why

the world is full of what theologians label "natural evil" such as tornadoes, floods, and earthquakes, and the devastation they inflict. Why is there "moral evil" such as people committing mass atrocities and individual perversions? The answer is a cursed world of fallen people living out their depraved natures. We are not intrinsically good, but morally twisted. The only solution for human society is a renewed nature, gradually restoring God's image in us, reformed into Christ's likeness.

The church is God's training ground for that divine project. It follows that churches should remain in a state of self-evaluation and continual reformation, asking themselves if their ministries are building people like Jesus Christ and reflecting that fruit into the world. Specific ministries that are not productive in one or both of those objectives should be reconsidered. Otherwise, we merely pursue our own religious schemes, missing God's intent to fix the mess.

The Ugliest Word

In any language, the ugliest and least popular word is "sin"—not the word itself but its meaning. Is it really true that within every human heart there lurks a spiritual sickness, a bias toward evil, a disposition toward error, a tendency toward wrong? It depends on who we ask and how we define the word.

According to the Bible, sin is real—nothing is more real than sin. Mankind's sin and God's plan of rescue from it is the central thread of the biblical story. And much of nonbiblical, human history records the reality of sin and its consequences. We daily observe sin's presence for we all swim in its waters. As Paul writes, We "all have sinned and fall short of the glory of God" (Romans 3:23). We try to deny or redefine it, but we cannot escape its ugly and terrible results. Sin may parade in individual form, such as murder, or in social form, such as racism, but it is unavoidable.

Through our history, many have defined sin from a nonbiblical slant. Some dismiss it as simply an illusion, or they call it ignorance or weakness, or massage it into psychological alienation, social maladjustment, oppression, or low self-esteem. The list of manmade definitions still grows. But the Bible, in simplest terms, calls sin lawlessness: "Everyone who sins breaks the law; in fact, sin is lawlessness" (1 John 3:4). The law in question is God's character, so anything inconsistent with God's character is sin.

The root idea of the biblical view of sin is deviation from God's character or the moral law that comes from it. Such deviation unveils itself in attitudes as well as actions, as seen in Jesus' teaching that sinful acts spring from within: "For out of the heart come evil thoughts, murder, adultery, sexual immorality, theft, false testimony, slander" (Matthew 15:19). So our alienation from God runs deeper than external behavior, broader than a few observable habits that some people find obnoxious.

Where did sin come from? It was introduced not by God, but by an angel, and then mankind, who both chose against God. The first sin was the desire of Lucifer (Satan) to be independent of God. Other angels joined the mutiny against their Creator. According to Paul, "Sin entered the world through one man" (Romans 5:12). When Satan deceived Eve, and she violated God's prohibition in the garden, then Adam knowingly joined her

41

SIN

145

rebellion. Thus we all became sinful through our connection to Adam.

The broad effect of sin is a state of alienation from God, specifically resulting in sin's slavery, guilt, death, and hell. Man is helpless to remove himself from this dilemma, but God provides deliverance in Jesus Christ. When He died on the cross He bore the penalty for our sin required by God's righteousness and justice. Sinful men and women are then forgiven sin's penalty and freed from sin's power by accepting by faith what Christ did for us. If you have never turned to Him for forgiveness and liberation, no time is better than now. Simply pray to God in faith, admitting that you have sinned, and telling God that you believe Christ died in your place to pay the penalty for your sins. The wording is not important, but genuine trust in Christ's provision for you is.

Rotten to the Core

Why is sin so widespread if we're essentially good, as we're often told? If we're sinful only because society corrupts us, we would expect centuries of attempted social improvement to make us better people. But history tells a different story. For instance, the twentieth century's high-tech benefits also elevated the means of human brutality to unprecedented levels. Our basic nature has remained unchanged for millennia. Where does our common evil come from?

Augustine coined the phrase "original sin" for the pervasive result of Adam's deed that infects us all. This total depravity depicts the universal effect of his rebellion against God on all his descendants (Romans 5:12,19). Original sin does not suggest: (1) We were created sinful. God created mankind morally pure and innocent (Ecclesiastes 7:29). Or, (2) the human reproductive process is sinful. David's comment about being "sinful from the time my mother conceived me" (Psalm 51:5) does not refer to his parents' physical union but the sinful nature that originates at conception.

Total depravity does not mean we're as bad as we can possibly be. We're not all Adolf Hitlers, and even Hitler could have been worse, as unimaginable as that seems. Total depravity means our every capacity (our mind, spirit, will, emotions, body) is tainted, and we can do nothing to alter or escape that condition. Few will match Hitler's atrocities, but "all have sinned and fall short of the glory of God" (Romans 3:23).

Paul ties Adam's sin to us in Romans 5:12, "Sin entered the world through one man, and death through sin, and in this way death came to all men, because all sinned." But how exactly does the responsibility for Adam's sin become ours? What is the connection? Two major theological systems, Arminianism and Calvinism, are divided in part by the answer.

Arminians believe we receive Adam's corrupted nature, but his guilt is removed from us as God applies to everyone a form of grace called "prevenient grace." We are thus enabled to choose the good and respond to God's salvation offer. Some Arminians even believe we can respond to God because our will is not fallen.

Following Augustine, Calvinists believe that God imputed to us both Adam's corrupted nature and his guilt. Some say Adam acted as our representative, meaning when he sinned he did so for us as well. Others believe we were genetically present in Adam and thus we actually sinned when he did. Either way, we're spiritually dead and therefore unable to respond to God.

The consequence of our sinful condition is that we don't become sinners when we sin; we sin because we already are sinners, and we need God's grace from start to finish. Only by His intervention can we begin to reverse the devastating effects of our fallen nature. Even though it will not be removed in this life, its power over us is broken so that we can choose against its influence.

Our Poisoned Capacities

Adam and Eve produced children only after the Fall. Consequently all their descendants inherit their fallen moral tendency—a natural inclination away from God and against His will. "No one living is righteous before [God]" (Psalm 143:2). "[A]ll have sinned and fall short of the glory of God" (Romans 3:23). Sin's effect is total, fundamentally inside the soul but overflowing into personal relationships, society, and the world.

The Fall poisoned every human capacity, so that all human nature is tainted by sin's infection. Our mind rejects God's truth (1 Corinthians 2:14); our emotions seek their own pleasure (Ephesians 2:3); our will chooses sin (Romans 7:15); our conscience approves immorality (Romans 1:32). Jeremiah identified the central problem: "The heart is deceitful above all things and beyond cure" (Jeremiah 17:9).

In the Sermon on the Mount, Jesus illustrated Jeremiah's point by saying observable sins like murder and adultery originate inside as hate and lust (Matthew 5:21-28). When teaching the Pharisees, Jesus repeatedly

SIN **43**

stressed that sin is an internal matter before it erupts externally (Matthew 23:25-28). Our real issue is not our upbringing, other people, the government, or the environment, but ourselves. We are our problem, and life's other tensions only manifest our deeper, internal breach with God.

Our God relationship is the hinge upon which all others turn. Alienated from Him, all other connections suffer—families, neighborhoods, churches, countries, and races. The outgrowth of our deformed spirit damages society at every level. Because the driving force behind all human motives, whether personal, corporate, or government, is now self, conflict is inescapable. Every fight, whether children at play or nations at war, originates within our nature before it reaches personal conflict and international politics.

Part of our sinfulness is our inability to see the real issue. When Jesus tutored Nicodemus about "flesh giv[ing] birth to flesh" (John 3:6), Nicodemus thought Jesus was teaching biology. But Jesus' lesson dealt with spiritual truth, saying morally fallen people produce children with the same twisted tendency, and thus we all need a new, spiritual birth.

Speaking for all of us, Paul reveals his powerlessness to free himself from his own sinful disposition (Romans

7:24). The solution is found only in Christ's payment for sin. When by His grace we appropriate His saving work, we die to sin and receive newness of life (Romans 6:1-4). The Holy Spirit now indwells us (Romans 8:9), empowering us to increasingly resist sin and live by Christlike traits (Galatians 5:22-24). Only then is sin restrained.

Most attempts to improve our world, whether individual, corporate, or international, aim at the secondary manifestations of the mess we're in. Unless we identify the core problem, our well-intentioned efforts are only a moral Band-Aid on cancer. It may look like we're doing something, and it may make us feel better temporarily, but the cancer continues to spread, leading to death. The church needs to be about God's business of bringing spiritual healing to a sin-sick world.

Universal Devastation

A society based on relativism claims that no act is wrong if it doesn't hurt anyone. But sin always hurts someone. Its aftermath is widespread and devastating. The sinner, society, and God Himself are affected. The result of sin is the most relevant, pressing, far-reaching issue we face in this fallen world. Most efforts of law enforcement, government, and education are attempts to reduce, correct, or avoid sin's consequences.

Sin's internal effect, where it first appears, is its addictive power (Romans 6:16). Specific addictions vary, but sin's grip enslaves us all. Its malignant growth spreads through the soul like a cancer without a cure. The experiential result of sin includes an unrelenting lack of contentment. Our sinful nature is insatiable, unlimited in its selfish capacities, always wanting more. But God made us with a hole in the soul only He can fill, and the temporary pleasures of sin are no substitute for what He alone can do.

Sin's judicial outcome is guilt and death. When the Bible speaks of guilt, it does not mean mere psychological

44

SIN

guilt feelings that can be alleviated by pop therapy, but true moral guilt from violating God's absolute standard, which only He can absolve (Psalm 32:5). Unforgiven sin leads to death (Romans 6:23), appearing in three forms:

1. Physical death—separation of soul and body which all humans will see (James 2:26)
2. Spiritual death—separation from God, which is the current status of all unbelievers (Ephesians 4:18)
3. Eternal death—the permanent condition of separation from God in a place the Bible calls hell, the final destiny for all who never receive Christ's liberation and new life (Luke 12:5)

Sin's effect inevitably strains and breaks relationships—personal, social, and global. As we pursue our self-centered concerns we grow calloused toward others, resulting in conflict, crime, and war. The authority of law provides some constraint on the worst of our sinful passions, but part of our inner corruption is a rebellious spirit that rejects any authority that would, in part, restrain our behavior. We need more than external restriction; we need internal transformation.

A broken relationship between us and God is sin's worst and most lasting result. Many people diminish or deny the gravity of sin, but God does not; He hates it. Because of our sin, the Bible pictures us as God's enemies (Colossians 1:21), positioned for His punishment rather than blessing. Because God is perfectly just and righteous He cannot disregard sin—He has to punish it. Otherwise, He would not be just, and there would be no justice.

We applaud the best efforts of politicians, teachers, and social workers, but the consequences of sin are so dreadful that God alone can fix them. His solution is Christ's payment for sin, leading to our dying to sin in union with Christ, and the indwelling Spirit transforming us into Christ's likeness. Sin's impact is massive, but God's grace is sufficient and available to all.

The Many Faces of Sin

An earlier generation of Christians described sin as a few habits they found personally offensive. But sin is more complex than a short list of social taboos. The Bible identifies three kinds of sin: imputed sin, inherited sin, and personal sin.

"To impute" means to charge something to an account as Abraham's faith was credited to him as righteousness (James 2:23). Since Adam's sin is credited to our account, it's called imputed sin (Romans 5:12). Because he's the head of the human race, we're each charged with the guilt of his sin. Imputed sin is not passed from generation to generation but applied directly from Adam to each of us. God erases our imputed sin, however, by charging it to Christ on the cross and crediting or imputing His righteousness to us (2 Corinthians 5:21).

We receive inherited sin, our sinful nature (Ephesians 2:3), through our parents' genes. David reveals that his sinfulness originated before he performed a single act. He was, in fact, "sinful from the time

SIN **45**

[his] mother conceived [him]" (Psalm 51:5). We are all born with this sinful tendency, but God's redemptive plan addresses this kind of sin also. "Those who belong to Christ Jesus have crucified the sinful nature with its passions and desires" (Galatians 5:24). Crucifixion does not mean our sinful nature no longer exists, but it no longer enslaves us. We "have been set free from sin" (Romans 6:18). We can submit to it if we so choose, but the indwelling Spirit is given to us to counter its influences: "Live by the Spirit, and you will not gratify the desires of the sinful nature" (Galatians 5:16).

A third kind of sin is personal sin—the acts, words, and thoughts we and others commit. The Bible includes several long and ugly lists of these sins. Consider the partial list in Galatians 5:19-21: "sexual immorality, impurity and debauchery; idolatry and witchcraft; hatred, discord, jealousy, fits of rage, selfish ambition, dissensions, factions and envy; drunkenness, orgies, and the like." "And the like" tells us that Paul could have extended the list, but he had made his point—the résumé of the fallen human nature is less than flattering. Personal sins cannot be blamed on Adam's first transgression or our parents' genes, but are the sins we ourselves commit. By means of Christ's death God makes available His forgiveness for these violations (Ephesians 1:7).

45 SIN

Provision for every kind of sin is available in Christ's saving work on the cross. Justice is not violated if a substitute willingly pays the condemned person's penalty, as Christ did. As our representative, Christ died in our place, receiving our punishment even though we were guilty of what He paid for. He has supplied exactly and fully what we need for our multiple sin problem.

By faith we receive His provision for us, and we live in newness of life. Our lives should now display the dominance of the indwelling Spirit rather than the sway of the sinful nature. As we learn and live God's Word, this transformation of inner influence progressively moves from our past pattern of sin toward God's glorious intent for us—Christlike character and behavior.

Leaning the Wrong Way

Most parents understand the sinful nature—their children unveil it daily. All are born with the inclination to do wrong—they need no tutoring to follow sin's path. Paul directed parents to curb that natural tendency by "bring[ing children] up in the training and instruction of the Lord" (Ephesians 6:4). The apostle's command reveals two things about the sinful disposition: (1) All children possess it; and (2) It can be modified.

Our sinful nature, sometimes called "the old man" or "the flesh," is not a part of the soul or body but a tendency—a self-centered bias to choose contrary to God and His will. Our natural capacities to think, feel, will, and act incline away from rather than toward God. We impulsively and intentionally pursue our own way instead of God's.

How did this universal human condition arise since God created Adam and Eve pure and innocent, without partiality for sin or rebellion (Genesis 1:27,31)? God also created them with the power of choice, which they used to rebel against God, resulting in their own corruption

46

SIN

(Genesis 3). They then reproduced offspring infected with the same constitution (Romans 7:5). Even among Christians, an internal struggle rages between the sinful nature and the Spirit: "For the sinful nature desires what is contrary to the Spirit, and the Spirit what is contrary to the sinful nature. They are in conflict with each other . . ." (Galatians 5:17).

The sin nature devastates everything—we are fully tainted and unable to satisfy God (Romans 7:18-20). Paul wrote that "the sinful mind is hostile to God. It does not submit to God's law, nor can it do so. Those controlled by the sinful nature cannot please God" (Romans 8:7-8). Jesus said we are even slaves to sin (John 8:34). All our relationships are impaired by this innate condition. The collective effect on society emerges as hatred and injustice between individuals, and war and genocide among nations and ethnic groups.

As dreadful as the results of the sinful nature are, the situation is not hopeless. Three influences provide some restraint on our drive toward sin: human conscience (Romans 2:14-15), family training (Proverbs 22:6), and government (Romans 13:1-7). Christians have additional, supernatural aid over the sin nature because it has been crucified with Christ (Galatians 5:24) and we are therefore no longer enslaved to it (Romans 6:6).

Spiritual birth gives us a renewed predisposition toward God, and as we grow spiritually we gain increasing victory over the old sin nature's power. As we "live by the Spirit, [we] will not gratify the desires of the sinful nature" (Galatians 5:16).

Jesus' freedom liberates us from the most brutal slavery of all—slavery to ourselves. When, by His grace and power, we no longer have to obey our passions, we know a freedom that cannot be enslaved by any external force. Referring to Himself He proclaimed, "You will know the truth, and the truth will set you free. . . . [And] if the Son sets you free, you will be free indeed" (John 8:32,36).

46 SIN

Neither Perfect nor Lawless

In Christ we die to the sin nature in that we are no longer its slaves (Romans 6:2,14). But we're still able to sin. So what happens when a Christian sins? Efforts to understand this issue have led to extremes—perfectionism in one direction and antinomianism (lawlessness) in the other. Perfectionism is the belief that the Christian can attain a state of sinlessness in this life. Antinomianism is the view that because the sin is already paid for, the Christian can sin without concern or restraint.

John's first letter excludes both extremes. According to 1:8, becoming a Christian does not imply a perfect life: "If we say that we have no sin, we deceive ourselves, and the truth is not in us" (NKJV). Nor, in the other direction, does salvation erase our obligation to keep moral standards as seen in 2:4-6: "The man who says, 'I know him,' but does not do what he commands is a liar, and the truth is not in him. . . . This is how we know we are in him: Whoever claims to live in him must walk as Jesus did."

So what does happen when a Christian sins? We should first emphasize that our legal status before God

SIN | **47**

remains unchanged: "There is now no condemnation for those who are in Christ Jesus" (Romans 8:1). Christ paid for our sins without distinction between past, present, and future sins (1 Corinthians 15:3). No Scripture hints that Christ's death atoned only for sins prior to our salvation but was ineffective for later sins. When we sin we are still justified in Christ—adopted children of God.

But, despite our security in Christ, our sin bears consequences. God is displeased like any father with a disobedient child. Our fellowship with Him is disrupted. "If we claim to have fellowship with him yet walk in the darkness, we lie and do not live by the truth" (1 John 1:6). Our sin also hinders the Spirit's aid and productivity in our lives (1 Thessalonians 5:19; Ephesians 4:30), impedes our spiritual growth (1 Peter 2:1-2,11), and brings God's discipline upon us (Hebrews 12:10-11; 1 Corinthians 11:28-32).

The basis for our forgiveness is the same as when we first came to the cross—Christ's blood. "The blood of Jesus, his Son, purifies us from all sin" (1 John 1:7). We appropriate His sin-bearing work by confessing that sin. "If we confess our sins, he is faithful and just and will forgive us our sins and purify us from all unrighteousness" (1 John 1:9). To confess means we call the sin what God calls it; we acknowledge it as sin rather than

47

SIN

deny or excuse it. Our fellowship with God is then restored.

The best way for the Christian to handle sin is to avoid it in the first place. Learning God's Word helps, "I have hidden your word in my heart that I might not sin against you" (Psalm 119:11). We are also supernaturally aided by the power of the indwelling Spirit (Galatians 5:16) and the prayers of our interceding Savior (Hebrews 7:25). But God's supernatural assistance does not remove our own responsibility to resist temptation (Hebrews 12:4), to say "no" when sin calls.

All but This One

Some people fear they've committed "the unforgivable sin" Jesus talked about in the Gospels (Matthew 12:31-32; Mark 3:28-29; Luke 12:10). Matthew's account reads, "And so I tell you, every sin and blasphemy will be forgiven men, but the blasphemy against the Spirit will not be forgiven. Anyone who speaks a word against the Son of Man will be forgiven, but anyone who speaks against the Holy Spirit will not be forgiven, either in this age or in the age to come."

So what is the unforgivable sin? Suggestions include murder, adultery, dying in unbelief, or some sin done only when Christ was on earth. But none of those appear to fit the passage. Murder and adultery are serious sins, but unrelated to Jesus' comment. David, in fact, committed both and was forgiven. It may be dying in unbelief, but Jesus seems to be talking of something more precise than generic unbelief. Perhaps it's something that can be committed only during the time of Jesus' earthly life, but the text doesn't actually say that. He called the unforgivable sin "blasphemy against the Holy

48

SIN

Spirit," an obvious warning about one's spiritual condition, but what does that mean?

The setting for Jesus' words was a controversy with the Pharisees over the source of Jesus' power to exorcize a demon from a man who was blind and could not speak. The Pharisees had already seen compelling proof of who Jesus really was, but they accused Him of working miracles by being in cahoots with Satan. Thus the Pharisees were attributing the work of God to the Devil, despite the evidence they had witnessed. Their problem was not blind ignorance, but willful rejection. That deliberate refusal to believe, even though knowing the truth, seems to be what Jesus called the unforgivable sin.

Why would that be unforgivable? If people accuse Jesus of being satanic even though they know He's the Christ, their inner state is so hardened they will not repent. Jesus apparently believed the Pharisees had done just that—they knew who He was, that His work was from the Spirit, yet they assigned it to Satan. Their hearts were hardened to the point of no potential repentance, meaning no forgiveness was possible. Because God was present and active in Christ, to reject Him was to reject God and any forgiveness available through Him. Jesus' words identified that rejection as final and irreversible. The unforgivability comes not from any lack in

God's grace, but from their determined choice to reject God's means of forgiveness.

If you're worried that you may be guilty of the unforgivable sin, you almost certainly are not. Concern about committing it reveals the opposite attitude of what the sin is. Those who might be guilty wouldn't care because they have no distress or remorse over the possibility. So the concern of those who fear they've committed the unforgivable sin is evidence they haven't. If you're reading this and care enough to reflect on the issue, you're probably not guilty.

48 | SIN

CHRIST'S PREINCARNATION

Before Jesus of Nazareth

Christ existed in eternity past before His birth as Jesus. He publicly proclaimed, "Before Abraham was born, I am!" (John 8:58), an obvious allusion to Jahweh's self-identification when Moses asked His name in Exodus 3:14. Christ never began but always was, and came to be one of us while still being what He was. "In the beginning was the Word, and the Word was with God, and the Word was God. . . . The Word became flesh and made his dwelling among us. We have seen his glory, the glory of the One and Only, who came from the Father, full of grace and truth" (John 1:1,14). The enfleshed Word dwelling among us was the Word eternally dwelling with the Father.

The importance of this doctrine can hardly be overstated. Christianity stands or falls on Christ's preexistence. If Christ began at Jesus' birth, He lied and is not eternal, thus not God, and no Trinity exists. The Jewish leaders understood the importance of Christ's claim to be the eternal "I Am." "At this, they picked up stones to stone him" (John 8:58-59), the punishment for blasphemy. Several lines of evidence argue for Christ's preexistence:

- His role in creation "[f]or by him all things were created" (Colossians 1:16)
- His divine traits "[f]or in Christ all the fullness of the Deity lives in bodily form" (Colossians 2:9)
- His being sent into time to execute God's redemptive plan since "when the time had fully come, God sent his Son, born of a woman, born under law, to redeem those under law" (Galatians 4:4-5)
- His prior glory with the Father which, anticipating His death, He asked to be resumed, "Father, glorify me in your presence with the glory I had with you before the world began" (John 17:5)

In addition to Christ's creative work, His preincarnate activity includes His recurring appearances as the Angel of the Lord (Genesis 22:11-18) and His special role with Israel in the Old Testament such as Paul's calling Him the "rock" of Exodus 17:5-7: "they drank from the spiritual rock that accompanied them, and that rock was Christ" (1 Corinthians 10:4).

The most stunning conclusion of Christ's preexistence is His uniqueness. He is set apart from all other religious leaders, completely different from all of them. He is the eternal God, one with the Father, who voluntarily chose to enter the world to reveal the Father: "No one has ever seen God, but God the One and Only, who is at the Father's side, has made him known" (John 1:18). Among the Bible's final words, which bluntly state His preexistence, Christ says: "I am the Alpha and the Omega, the First and the Last, the Beginning and the End" (Revelation 22:13).

Christianity is not just one option among many possibilities. We do not follow a mere religious leader or social revolutionary or miracle worker or wise teacher, but the one and only, eternal, Holy One. He is worthy of our praise, glory, and honor.

Remaining the Same, Becoming New

Our word "incarnation" comes from Latin, meaning "in flesh." It refers to the Second Person of the Trinity assuming a human nature without ceasing to be the eternal Son of God, thus becoming the God-man. This doctrine is the foundational fact of Christianity. The essential point may be summarized this way: "Remaining what he was, he became what he was not."[6]

That permanent, unique event differs from a theophany—a brief appearance of a divine Person in a visible form such as the burning bush in Exodus 3 or the Angel of the Lord in Judges 13. Christ forever became fully human while still being fully divine. The incarnation does not result in Jesus Christ being two persons possessing two identities and two wills in one body. He remains one person with two natures, one divine and one human.

That Jews were the first to believe this about Jesus shocks the mind. For centuries they had been raised to believe the oneness of God—and He wasn't human. Yet the New Testament authors, all Jews except Luke, focus above all on this event and its aftermath. Matthew introduces Jesus' divine reality at His birth, " 'The virgin will be with child and will give birth to a son, and they will call him Immanuel'—which means, 'God with us'" (Matthew 1:23). John pointedly says the divine Word became flesh, "In the beginning was the Word, and the Word was with God, and the Word was God. . . . The Word became flesh and made his dwelling among us" (John 1:1,14). Paul, the ultra-conservative Pharisee, reveals his theology of the incarnation by recording an early hymn about Christ: "Who, being in very nature God, did not consider equality with God something to be grasped, but made himself nothing, taking the very nature of a servant, being made in human likeness" (Philippians 2:6-7).

The history of heresies denying Christ's identity arose later. Ebionites denied Christ's preexistence and divine nature. Gnostics rejected His true humanity, even the reality of His body. Sabellians disbelieved the preincarnate existence of the Son of God. Arians said the Son's essence was not identical to the Father's. Apollinarians denied the full humanity of Christ's spirit. Monophysites believed Christ had only one nature.

Adoptionists rejected Jesus' deity until He was "adopted" by the Father at His baptism. Most modern deviations from the orthodox view of Christ are resurrected forms of these ancient heresies.

The historic debate over the incarnation has taken many turns, often leading to dead ends. But that does not lessen our need to explore the issue. More than academic matters are at stake. The kind of Savior we need, and if Jesus Christ is it, are the issues. The church has historically believed that Jesus Christ is the eternal Son sent by the Father to become fully man while remaining fully divine to be the mediator between God and man. Any view that gets it wrong is not Christian.

200 Percent Authentic

No mystery rivals the enigma of Jesus Christ—how He can be both God and man. The mystery includes several questions: Is He both deity and flesh? If He is both, how much of each nature, divine and human, does He possess? How do those natures relate to one another? Why is it important, if at all?

The concept of two natures in one person is called the hypostatic union. More important than the name, however, is the idea the name represents. But first, we need some background.

The early church included diverse groups who thought of Christ in different ways. Some thought He was God, but not really man—He only appeared to be human. Some thought He was man, but not fully God—He was missing some divine traits. Others thought He was a mixture of God and man—a sort of hybrid. For centuries, the early church wrestled within itself to express just what it did believe about this great mystery.

Finally, in A.D. 451, pastors and other church leaders gathered near Constantinople (modern Istanbul, Turkey) to discuss and record their understanding of the Bible's teaching on Christ's natures and person. In simplified form, their conclusion was that within the one person of Jesus Christ exist two distinct natures, one divine, one human. These natures are not mixed or diminished; each is complete. In other words Jesus Christ is not a 50-50 hybrid, half-man, half-God. He is now and forever 100 percent God and 100 percent man, without loss or mixture of any trait of either nature. He is one Person, truly and completely God, truly and completely man.

How and why could this be true? According to Philippians 2:6-7, in the incarnation the eternal Christ did not lose His deity, but added humanity. So His divine nature did not become less than the Father's or Spirit's divine nature. He simply added a human nature to His divine nature. He thus accepted certain limits on how He used His divine attributes so that He could execute the plan of salvation. He temporarily, voluntarily set aside the independent use and full display of His divine attributes and glory.

Theologian Millard Erickson uses the analogy of the world's fastest sprinter running a three-legged race with one leg tied to his partner. He still possesses all his natural speed, but he has temporarily, voluntarily restricted its use for the purpose of that race. He thus limits the outer expression of his full abilities.[7]

Is this complex issue just an intellectual toy for theologians with nothing better to do, or does it really matter? It's as important as our salvation. To be a mediator, a go-between, one must be acceptable or equal to both sides of a dispute. Thus, to mediate between God and man, Jesus Christ must be acceptable to both—fully God and fully man. We may not completely understand this great mystery, but we can be thankful for its reality. Our salvation rests upon it.

Christ's Emptying

In Philippians 2:7 Paul describes Christ's becoming man with the Greek word *kenoo*, "[He] emptied himself" (RSV). But what did the preexistent Son empty Himself of? Did He give up His deity, diminish His glory, surrender His divine self-awareness? Did He lose these, merely suspend them, or limit them in some other way? How and for how long did He "empty" Himself? What's involved in the Word becoming flesh?

The ancient church believed Christ deprived Himself of His glory while remaining divine. The medieval church so emphasized His divine nature that it almost neglected any self-limitation. After the Reformation, theologians began to think in terms of Christ setting aside the use of some divine attributes while still possessing them. In other words, Christ still had but hid His divine traits. The idea that Christ divested Himself of some or all divine qualities, therefore ceasing to be full deity, is new, not arising until the mid-nineteenth century.

This new view faces multiple problems. Textually, it's not supported by the best handling of Philippians 2:7.

And how could this view fit Jesus' mastery of nature as in Mark 4:39? "He . . . rebuked the wind and said to the waves, 'Quiet! Be still!' Then the wind died down and it was completely calm." Historically, it clashes with the church's Christology since the Council of Chalcedon (A.D. 451), when the church formalized its belief in two complete, undiminished natures of Christ. The new view's reluctance to believe in Christ's two natures reveals Monophysite tendencies, long ago rejected by the church as heresy. Functionally, reducing Christ's deity strips the world of its sustainer because He is "sustaining all things by his powerful word" (Hebrews 1:3) and "in him all things hold together" (Colossians 1:17). Logically, the new view results in the loss of the Trinity during the incarnation because one of the Persons does not qualify as deity throughout those thirty-three years.

The New International Version translates Philippians 2:6-7: "Who, being in very nature God, did not consider equality with God something to be grasped, but made himself nothing, taking the very nature of a servant, being made in human likeness." *Kenoo* is properly rendered "made himself nothing" because the translators recognize the New Testament's metaphorical use of the word. The passage does not say Christ stopped being divine, confirmed by Paul's words in Colossians 2:9, "For in Christ all the fullness of the Deity lives in bodily form." How Christ made Himself nothing was by "taking the very nature of a servant." He did not subtract anything, least of all His deity, but added something—servant-hood, thus becoming functionally subordinate to the Father during the incarnation. He still possessed His divine attributes and glory, but in humble obedience submitted their use and display to the Father's will.

Paul applies the doctrine for us: "Your attitude should be the same as that of Christ Jesus" (Philippians 2:5). If the eternal Son could humble Himself as described in those verses, how can we consider anything in life beneath us? If He could obey the Father to the point of suffering a horrible and undeserved death, how can we disobey in anything?

THE VIRGIN BIRTH

Supernatural Roots

Alex Haley's *Roots* touched a nerve in virtually everyone who watched it, not just African Americans, because all people want to know their heritage. But no one's lineage compares to Jesus'. The Bible says His mother conceived merely by the supernatural influence of the Holy Spirit without a man's involvement. No sexual contact occurred before the conception or birth because "[Joseph] had no union with her until she gave birth to a son" (Matthew 1:25). This does not imply a physical union between God and Mary, or an unusual delivery and birth as found in ancient mythologies.

Skeptics put forth pagan literature as the source of the Bible's virgin birth narrative. But the pagan myths lack the detailed, datable history and genealogies the New Testament provides (Matthew 1-2; Luke 1-3). For instance, Buddhist, Persian, and Babylonian birth stories occur in dreams or don't even mention a virgin birth. Other than the birth of a super-human person, pagan mythologies contain no similarity to the biblical account. And it's highly unlikely that Christian writers, especially

Luke, who boldly claimed careful historical research (Luke 1:3), would borrow from such dubious sources.

Other facts argue for the validity of the virgin birth account. First, the Hebrew character of both reports (Matthew 1:18-25 and Luke 1:26-38) indicates an early date for the story's origin, before pagan influences could have been absorbed into the record. Second, embellishing the facts would prove difficult while Mary was present to refute falsehoods.

We shouldn't be surprised if other New Testament books say little about the virgin birth. Their central message is Jesus' death and resurrection, not His origin, which naturally fits only the birth narratives. And early Christians may have refrained from public discussion of such a delicate matter related to Mary. Since the virgin birth matches the rest of the story of Jesus' miracles and resurrection, why should it seem strange that His earthly origin was supernatural? Would it not be more unusual if a miracle worker who returned from the dead had been conceived in the usual way?

Doubting the virgin birth exposes a deeper issue — the possibility of miracles at all. If one acknowledges that they could happen, the virgin birth is not unimaginable — certainly no more a miracle than the resurrection. To think otherwise does not refute the virgin birth as much as admit a bias against the possibility of any miracles, an admission that challenges the very existence or power of God. If God exists, is He unable to perform miracles? If He created the world, is He not able to send His Son into it through a virgin birth?

The practical importance of this doctrine goes to the center of our salvation. It illustrates that salvation comes from God's grace, not our works. It was His means of bringing into the world a Savior who was divine yet human, but not "in Adam" (Galatians 4:4; 1 Corinthians 15:22). The virgin birth also serves as a fairly reliable indicator of genuine Christianity. Those who reject it usually discard Christ's deity, His atoning work on the cross, salvation by faith alone, and obviously the inspiration and authority of Scripture. Removing the uniquely Christian doctrine of Jesus' "supernatural roots" leaves little to distinguish Christianity from generic, human religion.

The True Perfectionist

We call some people perfectionists, but they're not perfect, just demanding of themselves and sometimes others. Only one person is a true perfectionist, someone who's never sinned: Jesus Christ. The New Testament portrays Him as fully human, yet without sin. For two thousand years the church and even heretics have universally believed in His sinlessness (impeccability).

He claimed as much. He said He "always [did] what pleases [God]" (John 8:29). He even dared His opponents to "prove [him] guilty of sin" (John 8:46). None responded. Others announced His perfection. Paul refers to "him who had no sin" (2 Corinthians 5:21). Peter calls Him "a lamb without blemish or defect" (1 Peter 1:19) who "committed no sin" (1 Peter 2:22). John declares "in him is no sin" (1 John 3:5). Even Pilate confessed, "I find no basis for a charge against him" (John 18:38).

According to Hebrews 4:15, He met and resisted every temptation we face—physical, verbal, and mental: "For we do not have a high priest who is unable to sympathize with our weaknesses, but we have one who has been tempted in every way, just as we are—yet was without sin." But were His temptations real? The dilemma compares to the question: "Can an impregnable city be attacked?" Of course, but because it's impregnable it won't fall even though attacked with maximum force.

Jesus' wilderness encounter with Satan, often called "the great temptation," deserves special notice. Satan tried to steer Jesus away from relying on God and thus disqualify Him as the Messiah. But after forty days without food, without relying on His divine powers, Jesus resisted Satan's threefold offer: (1) to satisfy His hunger by turning stones to bread; (2) to receive power by submitting to Satan rather than God; and (3) to achieve fame by jumping from the peak of the temple to force God into a spectacular rescue (Matthew 4:1-11; Mark 1:12-13; Luke 4:1-13).

Peter's reference to Him as "a lamb without blemish or defect" (1 Peter 1:19) implies that if He had not been sinless, He would have been unable to pay for our sins and in need of a savior Himself. His sinlessness can be viewed from two sides: negatively, He never violated God's law; and positively, He always obeyed the Father, fulfilling the Law at every point. His sinless, obedient life qualified Him to be our sacrifice.

In addition to saving us from eternal death, He set

the example for earthly life. His refusal to sin is our model. "In your struggle against sin, you have not yet resisted to the point of shedding your blood" (Hebrews 12:4). Whatever struggles and temptations we face, we look to Jesus, and know we can resist for we've been told, "No temptation has seized you except what is common to man [including Jesus]. And God is faithful; he will not let you be tempted beyond what you can bear. But when you are tempted, he will also provide a way out so that you can stand up under it" (1 Corinthians 10:13).

CHRIST'S OFFICES

God's Bureaucracy

Bureaucracy curses modern life as government buries us beneath overlapping agencies and offices. God is more efficient, however, establishing just three offices in ancient Israel: the prophet to speak for Him to His people; the priest to offer Him sacrifices and prayers for His people; and the king to rule and protect His people. Christ's saving work is described by the same three offices: prophet (Deuteronomy 18:15; Acts 3:22), priest (Psalm 110:4; Hebrews 5:5-6), and king (Psalm 45:6; Luke 1:33).

Christ the prophet reveals God to us. He said, "Anyone who has seen me has seen the Father" (John 14:9). His prophetic role was unique because He was sent directly from God's presence, enabling Him to show the Father to us as no other prophet could (John 1:18). His unveiling work began before the incarnation as the eternal *Logos* bringing truth to the world (John 1:9), and it continues even now as His Spirit explains His word (John 14:26; 16:12-15). His complete revelation will occur when He returns and removes what hinders our current understanding (1 Corinthians 13:12).

Christ the priest reconciles us to God. According to Hebrews 9:14, He was both the sacrifice and the High Priest who offered the sacrifice. When He died, the temple veil in front of the Holy of Holies was torn in two (Luke 23:45) symbolizing our access to God. Through Him we can now draw near to God with confidence (Hebrews 10:19-22). His second priestly work was to enter "heaven itself . . . to appear for us in God's presence" (Hebrews 9:24). He remains at the Father's right hand because "he always lives to intercede for [us]" (Hebrews 7:25). When we sin He pleads our cause by presenting His righteousness as our justification.

Christ the King rules over us. The Old Testament pictures a king ruling forever from David's throne (Psalm 45:6-7; Isaiah 9:7), which Jesus called His own (Matthew 19:28). Even though not now acknowledged by all, God raised Him from the dead and then "seated him at his right hand in the heavenly realms, far above all rule and authority, power and dominion, and . . . placed all things under his feet and appointed him to be head over everything" (Ephesians 1:20-22). He now rules over those who accept Him as "the head of the body, the church" (Colossians 1:18), and one day His kingdom will be confessed by all (Romans 14:11).

Christ's three offices include practical application for us: When we study the Bible we learn the truth He prophetically revealed; when we pray we use the access to God He provided as priest; and when we serve, we take advantage of the safety His rule gives. In a small but Spirit-empowered way, we also reflect Christ's three functions. We are prophetic when we speak God's truth. We are a "royal priesthood" (1 Peter 2:9) who offer praise and good works as our sacrifice to God (Hebrews 13:15-16). We reign with Christ positionally even now (Ephesians 2:6), and we will rule experientially with Him in eternity (Revelation 22:5).

The Master Teacher

Even skeptics consider Jesus one of history's great teachers. He taught profound truth from the Father (John 7:16) in a simple yet authoritative style, covering the bits and pieces of this life and eternity (Matthew 7:28-29). The wise willingly learn from Him because He said His words will judge us all (John 12:48). Having come from the Father, He taught about God and His kingdom, Himself and His saving work, and mankind and morality.

Jesus taught that God is a living, loving, personal Spirit who created and sustains the universe. But, as a loving Father, He also provided for our needs (Luke 12:30-31). God judges but also offers His kingdom in Christ to whoever receives it. He portrayed God's kingdom not as a visible institution, but as God's active rule within those who submit to Him. The kingdom has therefore arrived in Christ (Luke 11:20) even though its fullness will not be seen until He returns (Matthew 13; Mark 13; Luke 21).

Jesus taught that He was the eternal Son (Matthew 11:27), sent by the Father "to give his life as a ransom for many" who were enslaved to sin (Mark 10:45). He informed the disciples that He was *the one* the prophets foretold: "We are going up to Jerusalem, and everything that is written by the prophets about the Son of Man will be fulfilled" (Luke 18:31). He contended that He did what His Father sent Him to do (John 17:4), revealed most clearly in His last comment on the cross, "It is finished" (John 19:30).

According to Jesus, God values us so much that He even counts the hairs of our head (Matthew 10:30). Contrary to the common view, Jesus said our value is not in what we have but what we are: "What good will it be for a man if he gains the whole world, yet forfeits his soul?" (Matthew 16:26). Consistent with this internal emphasis, He said defilement overflows from inside rather than corrupts from outside (Mark 7:14-23). Thus we need repentance and inner transformation (Matthew 4:17). His ethical teaching reinforces that theme—new life in Him alters motives instead of merely changing behavior (Matthew 5:21-22,27-28).

Jesus' other topics included the Holy Spirit, the church, and the future. He said He did what He did by the Spirit (Matthew 12:28), and after the Son was gone, the Spirit would continue His work by convicting the world (John 16:8), regenerating the lost (John 3:5-8), and teaching the saved (John 16:13). He introduced the church by telling Peter that Jesus would build His church upon the "rock" of Peter's confession of Jesus as the Christ (Matthew 16:16-19). His teaching about the future included His own return (Mark 13:26-27), our judgment (Matthew 12:36-37), and eternal destiny (Matthew 25:41,46).

Learning from Christ is more than academics. Paul commands, "Follow my example, as I follow the example of Christ" (1 Corinthians 11:1), requiring that we incorporate Christ's truth into our lives. When we submit to Christ's lordship we increasingly live by His teaching, displaying kingdom traits, and revealing our salvation to those who watch. As we approach our goal of becoming like Him, we treat others in love and grace as He did (Matthew 5:43-48).

The Cross of Christ

People wear crosses on T-shirts, tattoos, hats, and jewelry, symbolizing the Christian message, although few who wear it know that. The Greek word for *cross* means "a stake" and referred to a brutal form of capital punishment used by many ancient peoples. The earliest practice was simply impaling the victim on a sharpened pole. In time, two pieces of wood were joined to form a "T" or to extend the vertical pole above the crossbar like most crosses today.

After sentencing, the Romans forced the condemned person to carry the crossbeam to the execution site escorted by a squad of four soldiers and their centurion (John 19:17; Matthew 27:32). They preceded the crucifixion with scourging (John 19:1; Acts 22:24). (Jesus was apparently scourged before walking to the crucifixion site, because Simon of Cyrene was forced to carry His cross [Luke 23:26], suggesting that Jesus was unable to do so.) The victim's wrists were tied or nailed to the crossbeam (Luke 24:40), which was then hoisted up and attached to the vertical stake. The feet were secured, and a sign announcing the criminal's crimes displayed. After days of shock, thirst, and exposure, death came from asphyxiation as the muscles used for breathing failed.

Ancient authors rarely mentioned crucifixion. Their readers—the educated, cultured elite—viewed crucifixion with disgust as pornography might be viewed today. The gospel writers reflect the same reserve. Their accounts of Jesus' trial and death are remarkably detailed, but their record of His crucifixion is brief. All four simply write, "They crucified him" (Matthew 27:35; Mark 15:24-25; Luke 23:33; John 19:18).

Since these executions were public, crucifixion victims endured verbal abuse and social stigma (Mark 15:29). Only slaves and dangerous criminals were crucified; Roman citizens were exempt except for treason or military desertion. The Jews attached an additional stigma—anyone hung on a tree was cursed by God (Deuteronomy 21:23). So the Christian message of a crucified Messiah raised a special problem for Jews.

We find Jesus' crucifixion in the Roman and Jewish histories of Tacitus and Josephus as well as the four Gospels. By comparing their ancient facts with modern astronomical data, scholars date Jesus' crucifixion on April 7, A.D. 30 or April 3, A.D. 33. The location was outside Jerusalem on a hill called Golgotha, "the place of the skull." The legal charge brought against Jesus by the Sanhedrin, the ruling body of Israel, was insurrection, an intolerable crime in the Roman Empire (Luke 23:2,5). But God's plan was working through the Jewish and Roman politics to provide our salvation by Jesus' death (1 Corinthians 15:3).

The cross of Christ is the core of God's message (1 Corinthians 2:2); the ultimate symbol of God's love as He nailed our indictment of sins on it, thus canceling the charges against us (Colossians 2:14). Jesus used the cross to symbolize discipleship: "If anyone would come after me, he must deny himself and take up his cross and follow me" (Mark 8:34). His hearers understood— rejection and suffering followed those who followed Him. Today when someone wears a cross he parades the symbol of God's redemption. Those of us who know the meaning of the cross should live its truth in the presence of others. Do they see that in us—a willingness to suffer to follow Jesus?

God's Go-Between

When management and labor can't agree on a contract they call in a mediator, a go-between. He can bring together the alienated parties because he's acceptable to both sides. Without a mediator they remain separated, a strike follows, productivity stops, and no one is happy.

The Bible says we need a mediator between us and God because in our sinful state we're "hostile to God" (Romans 8:7). Because He is holy He must judge sin, and because we're all guilty His wrath is reserved for each of us (Romans 2:5). He cannot simply ignore His holiness or call off His wrath toward sin. We, or someone acceptable to Him, must receive the wrath we are due or His justice is violated.

Early in Bible history, Job cried out for "someone to arbitrate between [himself and God], to lay his hand upon us both" (Job 9:33). His desire came true, in part, when God revealed Himself and His Law through Moses' mediation (Exodus 20:18-22). For the next fourteen centuries the people of Israel related to God through two mediating offices: prophets who spoke God's word for

195

Him to the people (Jeremiah 1:7,17), and priests who represented the people to God through sacrifices (Hebrews 5:1).

Those roles, however, were temporary, and we need a permanent mediator. But that requires someone acceptable to us and to God, someone both human and divine. The Old Testament prophets and priests did not qualify—they were men, but not God. Paul identified this "mediator between God and men, the man Christ Jesus" (1 Timothy 2:5). Hebrews 8:6 compares Christ and His ministry to the Old Testament priests: "The ministry Jesus has received is as superior to theirs as the covenant of which he is mediator is superior to the old one."

Jesus Christ fulfilled the mediator functions of both prophet and priest. In Acts 3:22 Peter referred to Jesus as the prophet Moses spoke of in Deuteronomy 18:15, "The LORD your God will raise up for you a prophet like me from among your own brothers." As a prophet, Christ spoke for God because He came from God (John 1:18; 14:10). As a priest, He forever finished the sacrificial work. "Unlike the other high priests, he does not need to offer sacrifices day after day, first for his own sins, and then for the sins of the people. He sacrificed for their sins once for all when he offered himself" (Hebrews 7:27).

On the cross He became cursed for us, receiving

God's wrath in our place (Galatians 3:13), thus satisfying God's justice and making peace between us and God (Ephesians 2:16). As a result all church-age believers are priests (1 Peter 2:5,9) with direct access to God through Christ our High Priest (Romans 5:1-2; Ephesians 2:18). In contrast to the beliefs of Roman Catholicism, we find no access through angels, deceased saints, clergy, or Mary because they cannot mediate for us. As God's people, we're to trust Christ as priest and learn from Him as prophet. We then act as human mediators offering His peace to others.

CHRIST'S ASCENSION AND SESSION

Up, Up, and Away

General Eisenhower led the World War II allies to victory in Europe. But his highest position of honor and power came when he was inaugurated President. In a rough parallel, the climax of Christ's earthly life was not His victorious resurrection but His ascension, His bodily transition from earth to heaven to rule from God's right hand, called His session.

David anticipated Christ's ascension in Psalm 68:18, "When you ascended on high, you led captives in your train," and His session in Psalm 110:1, "The LORD says to my Lord: 'Sit at my right hand until I make your enemies a footstool for your feet.'" Jesus prepared His disciples by saying, "Do not hold on to me, for I have not yet returned to the Father. Go instead to my brothers and tell them, 'I am returning to my Father and your Father, to my God and your God.'" (John 20:17). Forty days after His resurrection they witnessed His ascension from the Mount of Olives (Acts 1:3,9,12; Mark 16:19; Luke 24:50-51) as "he was taken up before their very eyes, and a cloud hid him from their sight" (Acts 1:9).

Paul taught this doctrine in 1 Timothy 3:16 and Colossians 3:1. Note also Ephesians 4:8-10, "'When he ascended on high, he led captives in his train and gave gifts to men.' (What does 'he ascended' mean except that he also descended to the lower, earthly regions? He who descended is the very one who ascended higher than all the heavens, in order to fill the whole universe)."

The author of Hebrews used the ascension and session to encourage faltering Jewish Christians (1:3; 9:24). He directly applied it to them in 4:14, "Therefore, since we have a great high priest who has gone through the heavens, Jesus the Son of God, let us hold firmly to the faith we profess." They needn't return to their Judaism because Christ's ascension and session prove His superiority over King David and even the angels (Acts 2:33-36; Hebrews 1:13). As the glorified God-man, He is now endowed with universal glory and honor "at the right hand of the throne of God" (Hebrews 12:2) even more than before His incarnation (Hebrews 2:9).

Christ's ascension and session benefit Christians in several ways. He's preparing a place for us (John 14:2). Based on our union with Him, we share in His session because we're seated with Him in the heavenly realms (Ephesians 2:6). He intercedes for us as our heavenly advocate (Romans 8:34; 1 John 2:1). Through Him we have continual access to God's throne (Hebrews 4:14-16). He pours out the Holy Spirit upon His church (Acts 2:33; John 7:39). His session points to and reminds us of His final triumph when He returns to judge (Acts 17:31; Romans 2:16).

Christ has won the cosmic battle and has been accepted by the Father. His entrance into heaven assures us that we will enter heaven. Because He is now and forever with us (Matthew 28:20), He always strengthens and protects us. We should draw enormous encouragement from this truth—He has won, and in Him we have won. Our destiny has been secured by our conquering hero, the ascended Christ, seated at God's right hand.

It's All About Choices

Some people say the point of life is making choices. Everyone enjoys choosing, and the Bible says God chooses. He selects or elects things for Himself. Some of His choices include Israel as a special nation (Acts 13:17), individuals for certain purposes such as David to be Israel's king (1 Samuel 16:7-12), and some people to salvation (Ephesians 1:4,11).

Election to salvation is God's choice, based on His grace. Out of His mercy and love, prior to creation and for His glory, God chose some to be saved, and determined they would be. This choice was based on nothing in the elect, but merely God's pleasure. His election, therefore, logically precedes their faith, "For he chose us in him before the creation of the world to be holy and blameless in his sight. In love he predestined us to be adopted as his sons through Jesus Christ, in accordance with his pleasure and will—to the praise of his glorious grace, which he has freely given us in the One he loves" (Ephesians 1:4-6).

Some believe that election to salvation is conditional,

based on our response, thus determined in part by us. In that view, God's election depends on our faith because He saves those He knew in advance would believe. Their salvation is determined—at least prompted—by their faith, which logically precedes God's election.

Like many doctrines about God's ways, election includes mystery. Some might rank this issue as the greatest paradox of all. We don't know why He chose those He did, or why He chose some instead of all or none. Nor do we fully understand how obeying the Great Commission (Matthew 28:19-20) or praying for the lost can mesh with God's election. But we learn from Jesus that the ultimate choice is God's, not ours, even though we make a real decision for which He rightly holds us responsible. As confounding as it is, those who come to Him are responding to His initiative, not their own. "You did not choose me, but I chose you" (John 15:16); and "No one can come to me unless the Father who sent me draws him" (John 6:44).

"That's not fair," some reply. From the human perspective, that's a legitimate reaction. But God is not obligated to save any. He is bound only by His justice, and He's not unjust by passing over some. Indeed He would still be just if He left all of us to pursue our own path of sin and death. But because His just demands against sin have been met by Christ, He's free to apply Christ's atoning work to whom He chooses—all, or none, or some. Whatever His reasons for applying it to some, He's not unjust in doing so.

Scripture doesn't teach election to tie us into doctrinal knots, but to amplify the greatness of God's grace and elevate our praise of Him who saves. The doctrine comforts us because we are "confident . . . that he who began a good work in [us] will carry it on to completion" (Philippians 1:6). We don't always know who are elect, but Jesus gave a clue—we will know them by their fruit (Matthew 7:16,20). Peter concludes that we should "be all the more eager to make [our] calling and election sure" (2 Peter 1:10). In response to this great doctrine, we should always praise Him who saved us by His mercy alone.

"Amazing Grace"

John Newton's classic hymn "Amazing Grace" is one of the world's most loved songs. But grace is more amazing than we know. "Grace" means a favor or gift—something given without being earned. Theologically, it means the undeserved gifts God gives us. Grace is, therefore, not a substance, a quantity of something we collect, but God's attitude that acts on our behalf without our deserving it. That absence of deserving or earning is the central idea of grace.

Grace first appears right after the Fall, in God's promise of a redeemer (Genesis 3:15). Later, God almost defines grace when describing Himself to Moses as "the compassionate and gracious God, slow to anger, abounding in love and faithfulness" (Exodus 34:6). In the New Testament, grace takes full expression, embodied in Jesus Christ, God's promised redeemer (John 1:14,17). Christ's death on the cross paid for our sins, clearing the way for God's grace to be offered without compromising His justice and righteousness (Titus 3:7; Romans 3:26).

Theologians divide grace into two big categories

called common and special. The first is called common because it's common to all. It refers to God's universal gifts such as providing basic needs, restraining evil, delaying judgment, and maintaining order. Special grace is given only to God's elect. It speaks of what God does to redeem, sanctify, and glorify His people. It includes enlightening their minds to understand the gospel, convicting their hearts of the need to believe it, and quickening their wills to accept it.

Theologians look at special grace from four angles.

1. *Prevenient grace* emphasizes that God's grace comes first. He initiates without our prompting or merit—the very point of grace. "We love because he first loved us" (1 John 4:19), and "While we were still sinners, Christ died for us" (Romans 5:8).

2. *Efficacious grace* means it accomplishes what God intended. No one can derail the Almighty's plan to save. As Jesus said, "All that the Father gives me will come to me . . . I give them eternal life, and they shall never perish . . . My Father, who has given them to me, is greater than all; no one can snatch them out of my Father's hand" (John 6:37; 10:28-29).

3. *Irresistible grace* proceeds from efficacious grace—it cannot be rejected to the end. Despite temporary struggles against God, He woos and eventually wins

the elect. Because God gives His people a new heart to know Him, they recognize and respond to His voice and follow Him (Jeremiah 24:7; John 10:27).

4. *Sufficient grace* means it's enough to achieve God's intent of saving those He chose. "Therefore [Christ] is able to save completely those who come to God through him" (Hebrews 7:25).

Even after salvation, His grace is sufficient for us (2 Corinthians 12:9), but growing in grace is a divine-human partnership. In other words, being saved by grace does not authorize a passive Christian life. Post-salvation grace excludes merit, not effort. Paul directly says that Christians work as God works in us (Philippians 2:12-13). One practical consequence of God's grace in us is our treating others graciously. We extend God's mercy and kindness to them whether they deserve it or not. The result is that all who watch us should see God's grace reflected in us.

Two Births

Every parent knows that nothing compares to the thrill of a child's birth. We marvel at the miracle of what we've made. We understand the basic biology, but mystery still surrounds this new life. More mysterious is the wild notion of being born twice. On the surface, that sounds crazy. Jesus raised the idea with an Old Testament scholar named Nicodemus, but Nicodemus was baffled, confusing the two births. "'How can a man be born when he is old?' Nicodemus asked. 'Surely he cannot enter a second time into his mother's womb to be born!'" (John 3:4). Nicodemus may have wondered if the young Rabbi was nuts.

Our phrase "born again" comes from Jesus' and Nicodemus' conversation (John 3:1-21). But what does it mean? This second birth is God's mysterious implanting of spiritual life in us, the transition from spiritual death to spiritual life. At that moment we become a "born again Christian," a redundant phrase because rebirth is the entrance into Christianity and God's kingdom (John 3:3). There are no "un-born again Christians." The theological term is "regeneration," which means a new beginning or rebirth.

Regeneration is entirely God's work. "God . . . made us alive with Christ even when we were dead in transgressions" (Ephesians 2:4-5). Despite the mystery that surrounds the second birth, this makes perfect sense. The subjects of birth, physical or spiritual, cannot give life to themselves; birth happens to them. John stressed this when describing God's children as "children born not of natural descent, nor of human decision or a husband's will, but born of God" (John 1:13). The flip side of regeneration being God's work is that it's not our work. We're spiritually dead, and dead people don't do anything. We don't plan our birth; we don't initiate it; we don't accomplish it. We don't choose to be born or even cooperate with God in our physical or spiritual birth.

But, someone may ask, "Don't I believe in Christ to be born again?" Yes and no. We really do believe, but not until we're alive. Chronologically, from our perspective, being born again and believing are simultaneous. But logically, our rebirth precedes our belief because there's no "I" to believe until "I" am alive. God sparks us to life so that we can express faith, which He gives us anyway.

New birth is the beginning, not the end of God's purpose for us. It results in new life, and that life must grow.

Ironic how we may claim some role we don't have in our birth, but then become casual about the role we do have in our growth. That's like a baby taking credit for birthing himself, but then not doing what's needed to grow up.

Be sure you've been born twice. Do you see evidence of spiritual life, such as the fruit of the Spirit (Galatians 5:22-23)? Be sure you're growing your spiritual life. Are you practicing spiritual disciplines like solitude and silence with God, study and meditation on His Word, confession and worship, fellowship and service with other saints? If we neglect those time-honored disciplines of the Spirit, we limit our spiritual growth.

Sorry, I Changed My Mind!

We all know what it is to change our mind, maybe every day. We may plan on pizza for lunch and drive toward the pizza place but decide on tacos instead. The inner change of mind changes our outer action. The common "What's for lunch?" scenario illustrates biblical repentance. The usual Hebrew word for repentance meant to turn the other way. The common Greek word meant to change one's mind, leading to a change of action. The theological significance is the inner turning from sin to God, resulting in a changed life.

People often confuse "repentance" with emotion. But emotional grief does not guarantee real repentance. It might be no more than distress over lost blessing or feared punishment. Biblical repentance may include emotion but it goes much deeper—it turns from one path to another. Stated differently, false repentance *feels*; genuine repentance *acts*. Paul distinguishes between mere sorrow and true repentance in 2 Corinthians 7:9, "You were made sorry, but . . . your sorrow led . . . to repentance." So biblical repentance is an attitude change that reveals itself in how we live.

Repentance and faith are inseparable. Repentance is the negative side, faith the positive side, of turning from sin to Christ. We distort the biblical picture if we assume we can have one without the other. Paul integrates both when summarizing his gospel message in Acts 20:21: "I have declared to both Jews and Greeks that they must turn to God in repentance and have faith in our Lord Jesus." When Peter described the Gentiles' coming to saving faith, the other apostles called it "repentance unto life" (Acts 11:18).

We don't manufacture repentance—it comes by God's enablement. Second Timothy 2:25 says, "God will grant them repentance leading them to a knowledge of the truth." In His sovereign grace God initiates repentance in us because we cannot do it on our own. Sin is so rooted within that Jeremiah maintains we can no more turn from it than an Ethiopian can change his skin color or a leopard change its spots (Jeremiah 13:23).

We usually associate repentance with unbelievers coming to salvation, but the Bible cites a repentant spirit among believers. Consider Paul's instructions to the Ephesian Christians: "With regard to your former way of life . . . put off your old self . . . to be made new in the attitude of your minds; and . . . put on the new self"

(4:22-24). Repentance should be the believer's response when the Spirit convicts of sin. We express our repentant attitude through confession, and the Spirit forgives and restores us to fellowship (1 John 1:9).

Whole churches can repent as the Lord commanded the Ephesian and Laodicean churches (Revelation 2:5; 3:19). Considering the state of the Western church today, the time has come for our repentance. Like the churches in Ephesus and Laodicea, we should turn from our spiritual apathy and to Christ and His Word, resulting in changed lives. May we ask God to give us that repentant spirit individually and corporately.

Total Trust

Some people treat faith as belief in nothing, wishful thinking, what they call "blind faith." Blind faith, however, has no place in Christianity, which is founded on solid evidence and sound reasoning. Peter addresses this very issue in 2 Peter 1:16: "We did not follow cleverly invented stories when we told you about the power and coming of our Lord Jesus Christ, but we were eyewitnesses of his majesty." Eyewitness accounts are not the stuff of blind faith.

The topic of faith raises three big questions. First, *What is saving faith?* This issue is no small matter since James 2:14 describes a kind of faith that does not save. "What good is it . . . if a man claims to have faith but has no deeds? Can such faith save him?" The Reformers identified three ingredients in saving faith: (1) Knowledge of the gospel. Saving faith is not faith in nothing; it's directed at the person and work of Christ. One must know the facts to be saved. (2) Agreement with those facts. If someone knows the information but considers it false, she obviously does not possess saving faith.

(3) Personal trust in those facts. I rely or depend on Jesus' death to pay the penalty for my sin. Saving faith includes all three elements—knowledge, agreement, and trust.

The second big question is, *What is the linkage between faith and reason?* Church history offers three positions: (1) Reason precedes faith. In this view the intellect is all-important, and faith is only a function of reason. (2) Faith and reason oppose one another. Faith is ultimate, and reason is the enemy which faith must conquer. (3) Faith precedes and enables reason. In other words, both faith and reason are necessary and work together. This third stance fits best with Scripture, which portrays faith and reason as interwoven parts of our whole person. God created us with rational minds to process information He reveals. Our response of faith is integrated with that information which our minds process.

The third big question is, *What is the relationship between faith and works?* Paul addresses this issue head on: "It is by grace you have been saved, through faith—and this not from yourselves, it is the gift of God—not by works" (Ephesians 2:8-9). God justifies based on Christ's imputed righteousness, which we accept by faith rather than earn by deeds (2 Corinthians 5:21; Romans 3:20,24; 4:3).

Some conclude that justification by faith, apart from works, renders works unimportant. But the Bible says otherwise: "We are . . . created in Christ Jesus to do good works" (Ephesians 2:10). Genuine saving faith always produces deeds, which show that our claim to faith is real (James 2:14-26). Works, therefore, have their place. The issue is timing—they follow rather than precede salvation, giving evidence that our faith is genuine.

God is not blind to our post-salvation works. He promises us rewards in heaven (Philippians 3:12-14; 2 Timothy 4:7-8). Christians should, therefore, demonstrate our faith by deeds that result in heavenly rewards for us and eternal glory to God. Like God, Christian faith is neither blind nor lazy.

Just Charge It

If you buy a CD with my credit card, you're charging that purchase to my account. No cash changes hands but a real financial transaction occurs. So, charging something refers to a legal accounting process. God's plan of salvation uses a similar image. Our theological word "imputation" or "to impute" comes from a Latin word that refers to recording a transaction on a ledger; charging something to that account. The Bible uses that accounting image for salvation in three ways.

First, Adam's sin was charged or imputed to everyone in the human race. God then counts you and me guilty and deserving of Adam's punishment because Adam's sin was charged to our accounts. As Paul writes in Romans 5:18-19, "The result of one trespass was condemnation for all men. . . . Through the disobedience of the one man the many were made sinners."

Second, our sin and guilt were imputed to Christ on the cross. God thought of our sin as belonging to Christ, and Christ paid for it by His death. The Old Testament sacrifices anticipated Christ doing this. The sins of the person offering the sacrifice were transferred to the sacrificial animal that temporarily paid for those sins by its death. God could then forgive the offerer. Isaiah spoke in 53:6 of Christ's sacrifice that would be the permanent payment for our sin, "The LORD has laid on him the iniquity of us all." Paul writes of this in 2 Corinthians 5:21, "God made him who had no sin to be sin for us."

Third, Christ's righteousness is imputed to the believer's account. According to Romans 3:10, "There is no one righteous, not even one." In God's eyes we are all unrighteous. But God imputes Christ's righteousness to every believer's account. In 2 Corinthians 5:21 Paul adds this third aspect of imputation to the second, "God made him who had no sin to be sin for us, so that in him we might become the righteousness of God." God now thinks of Christ's righteousness as ours. Having credited us with Christ's righteousness, God can pardon us and call us righteous.

Our new status in God's eyes is not based on any actual condition of righteousness in us but on Christ's imputed righteousness that God considers ours. Because imputation does not infuse us with righteousness, our internal character is unchanged by imputation. Imputation refers only to God's crediting Christ's righteousness to our account, not our acquiring righteousness in our nature. That righteous character is developed over time through spiritual growth resulting from the sanctification process.

God does not regard any human effort or merit when imputing Christ's righteousness to us. Therefore, the entire salvation process is based on His love, not our actions. Praise God for His mercy to give us what we don't deserve.

God's Pardon

Modern courts use DNA evidence to convict or acquit the accused. We even hear of inmates acquitted and released based on newly discovered DNA evidence. That legal picture illustrates the doctrine of justification, but with one caution. Our modern sense of acquittal usually means the accused did not commit the crime. Biblical justification is more like a pardon that doesn't hint that we never sinned, but still frees us because someone else paid the penalty we rightly deserve. In other words, God did not err by charging us with sin we're not guilty of. We rightly stand before His justice, but He commutes our sentence because Christ paid it.

Justification is God's declaration that we are righteous in His sight. The Greek legal word *dikaioo* means "justify," the opposite of "condemn." Paul makes that contrast in Romans 8:33-34, "It is God who justifies. Who is he that condemns?" Justification is more than forgiveness, which would make us only neutral in God's eyes; it declares us righteous as well. The basis for this divine pronouncement is God's placing our punishment on Christ and imputing Christ's righteousness to us. Because Christ's righteousness really is credited to us, justification is not a word game whereby God pretends we're something we're not. God did not ignore His righteous demands, but met them in Christ. He remains just while justifying us (Romans 3:25-26).

We receive God's gracious justification by faith alone (Romans 3:22; 5:1; Galatians 2:16). "For we maintain that a man is justified by faith apart from observing the law" (Romans 3:28). Our faith is not a meritorious act that deserves justification from God. Such "faith" would be a work, and works obligate God to pay us the wages we earn (Romans 4:4). Faith is merely the instrumental means by which we accept Christ's meritorious work (Romans 4:23-25).

What about the alleged contradiction between Paul and James regarding faith and works? (Romans 3:28, "A man is justified by faith apart from observing the law." James 2:24, "A person is justified by what he does and not by faith alone.") Because they are refuting opposite attacks on the gospel, we sometimes confuse ourselves by comparing those passages. Paul is condemning legalism that says we're saved by keeping the Law. James is denouncing spiritual anarchy that ignores Christian ethics. So Paul and James use the word "works" for different concepts. Paul means *works* as in obeying the Law of Moses to gain salvation. Since we're not saved that way, he condemns "works." James means *works* that result from our saving faith. Because they verify that our faith is real, he praises "works." The apostles complement rather than contradict one another. Our claim to saving faith (Paul) is verified by our visible works (James).

Justification is the most practical issue of all because it addresses how we can be acceptable to God. "Therefore, since we have been justified through faith, we have peace with God through our Lord Jesus Christ" (Romans 5:1). Justification is God's announcing His irrevocable judgment day verdict now. "Since we have now been justified by his blood, how much more shall we be saved from God's wrath through him!" (Romans 5:9). God has traded our guilt and punishment for Christ's righteousness, and we are forever secure with a hope, joy, and confidence we can never lose.

God's Cover-Up

Unlike other world religions, Christianity centers on the death rather than the teaching of its founder. Christians believe that Christ's death was not an accident of history, a tragic end to a botched Roman trial instigated by His opponents among the Jewish leadership. Rather, His death is the climax of God's plan to make amends or "atone" for our sin.

The original Hebrew word for atonement meant "to cover or cancel," thus the theological concept of erasing sin. We need this because the entire human race was hopelessly condemned when Adam sinned. "As for you, you were dead in your transgressions and sins . . . without hope and without God in the world" (Ephesians 2:1,12). Paul proclaims to all that "the wages of sin is death" (Romans 6:23).

The need for atonement originates in God's character because His justice is violated if forgiveness is offered without payment for sin. Therefore everyone will get his divine due. The provision of the atonement also comes from God's character because His love offered His own

Son as the payment. So the atonement displays God's justice, which required sin's payment, and His love, which met the demand.

Just as no tension exists between God's justice and love, no tension exists between the Father and the Son. Christ was not a grudging participant in a plan concocted by the Father alone. Christ said, "The good shepherd lays down his life for the sheep. . . . No one takes it from me, but I lay it down of my own accord" (John 10:11,18). Nor did the Son circumvent God's wrath that the Father was just itching to pour out on us. To the contrary, Paul tells us, "God was reconciling the world to himself in Christ" (2 Corinthians 5:19). The Father was the merciful provider of Christ, the willing, obedient sacrifice.

By His obedience, active and passive, Christ was qualified to be the atoning sacrifice. His active obedience was His perfect life that fulfilled the Law's demands. His passive obedience was His death on the cross that paid sin's penalty. A central theme of His death is substitution. He died in our place, as Isaiah explains, "He poured out his life unto death, and was numbered with the transgressors. For he bore the sin of many, and made intercession for the transgressors" (Isaiah 53:12). Christ acted as high priest who offered a sacrifice, but the sacrifice was Himself (Hebrews 9:11-15). And unlike those priests who repeatedly offered the animals, Christ offered Himself once, and it was fully and forever effective, "because by one sacrifice he has made perfect forever those who are being made holy" (Hebrews 10:14).

Because we are fallen and spiritually dead, we can do nothing to meet our need. But our sins are fully paid by Christ, and His righteousness is credited to us. We merely receive His work by faith. Furthermore, since God originates and completes the atonement, we can do nothing to undo it. God's wrath will never be directed at us. We are permanently secure in Christ. Never take for granted our costly salvation, but thank God for His mercy as we live lives fully devoted to Him.

Justice Served

When a person commits a crime, payment is required, often time in jail. After the sentence is complete, the legal system is satisfied and the prisoner set free. That human legal setting parallels God's salvation project described by the doctrines of expiation and propitiation. Expiation is the payment for sin required by guilt, thus freeing the sinner from sin's debt. Propitiation means the one sinned against is satisfied with the payment and turns away from wrath.

The idea is not mere cancellation of sin, which could be arbitrary forgiveness based on a whim. Rather, judgment is averted because Christ took the punishment in our place—intentional substitution stressed by both Old and New Testaments. "We all, like sheep, have gone astray, each of us has turned to his own way; and the LORD has laid on him the iniquity of us all" (Isaiah 53:6). "God made him who had no sin to be sin for us, so that in him we might become the righteousness of God" (2 Corinthians 5:21).

To fully understand this concept we must remember

God's nature. A holy, just, and righteous God cannot dismiss sin any more than an honest judge can ignore crime. Such a violation of justice would disqualify the judge from the bench. Likewise, God's holy wrath must address sin, or He's no longer holy and no longer God. But Paul assures us that God does His job: "The wrath of God is being revealed from heaven against all the godlessness and wickedness of men" (Romans 1:18).

God's plan to save does not violate His justice. By pouring His wrath on Christ, God satisfies His justice, thus preserving His character. He remains just even as He justifies us. "God presented [Christ] as a sacrifice of atonement . . . so as to be just and the one who justifies those who have faith in Jesus" (Romans 3:25-26). Furthermore, the salvation plan is not bribery because God Himself, motivated by love, provides the payment that satisfies His own demands. "This is love: not that we loved God, but that he loved us and sent his Son as an atoning sacrifice for our sins" (1 John 4:10). Christ's death did not change God from an angry God to a loving God—He was and is always both.

As a result of these doctrines we must face some profound questions. Do you believe Christ's death was sufficient to satisfy God's wrath, or must you add something to make up for what it lacked? If God wasn't satisfied with the death of His Son, what could we possibly do to make up the difference? For the Christian, can anything undo Christ's work that provides our salvation? The barrier our sin created between us and God has been removed. Christ freed us from the burden of debt we owed God. The price of our guilt has been paid in full, satisfying the Judge, who pardons us when we accept it by faith. We should always rejoice over God's grace, love, and mercy on our behalf. No trials of life can take that joy away.

It's Long Gone

Some people think all religions are the same. If we just explore the surface, we'll observe similar beliefs. But an honest comparison exposes significant disparities, even in the basic ideas. For instance, the concept of forgiveness is unique to Christianity and Judaism. Among the world's sacred books, the Bible alone teaches that an infinite, personal God completely forgives sin. And His forgiveness is not grudging or halfhearted. God says, "I will heal their waywardness and love them freely, for my anger has turned away from them" (Hosea 14:4).

The Hebrew and Greek words for forgiveness mean to cover an offense, or take away, put aside, let go of sin. Forgiveness relieves the resentment that comes from being wronged, thus restoring the relationship. Theologically, forgiveness is God's act of releasing sinners from judgment. In the Christian sense, forgiveness is always offered from God's initiative, and He's the only one who can forgive sins (Luke 5:21).

Forgiveness originates from within God's character because He is "a forgiving God, gracious and compassionate, slow to anger and abounding in love" (Nehemiah 9:17). But God is also free. He doesn't have to forgive sin; it's not automatic. Furthermore, His justice requires payment for sin. In other words, God wants to forgive but cannot without satisfying His justice. That's why the Old Testament priests offered sacrifices. "In this way the priest will make atonement for them, and they will be forgiven" (Leviticus 4:20). But those sacrifices were only a symbol of the permanent sacrifice revealed in the New Testament.

In Mark 2 Jesus shocked the crowds, when "he said to the paralytic, 'Son, your sins are forgiven'" (verse 5). The religious leaders understood the implications, and asked themselves, "Why does this fellow talk like that? He's blaspheming! Who can forgive sins but God alone?" (verse 7). Their theology was flawless; but they couldn't bring themselves to draw the right conclusion—this Jesus was God. He could pronounce forgiveness because He was God and the sacrifice for sin (Hebrews 9:15). His death was the permanent sacrifice which "destroyed the barrier, the dividing wall of hostility" between man and God (Ephesians 2:14).

Forgiveness is not the whole of God's salvation plan, but is an essential part of the gospel message: "Repent, then, and turn to God, so that your sins may be wiped out" (Acts 3:19). Even when a Christian sins, forgiveness is available through confession (1 John 1:9) because Christ "canceled the written code, with its regulations, that was against us and that stood opposed to us; he took it away, nailing it to the cross" (Colossians 2:14).

Forgiveness is more than a salvation issue. Paul tells us, "Forgive whatever grievances you may have against one another. Forgive as the Lord forgave you" (Colossians 3:13). And the Lord said our forgiveness should be limitless (Matthew 18:21-22). God will disburse whatever justice needs conveyed, "'It is mine to avenge; I will repay,' says the Lord" (Romans 12:19). By not holding bitterness or bearing grudges, we confirm the gracious character of our forgiving God.

Purchased from the Slave Market

Slavery was common in ancient cultures. The sale and purchase of this human commodity occurred at markets — slave markets. In the New Testament era, slaves made up a large part of the Roman Empire's population, as high as one third in Italy. These public transactions were common sights, so everyone knew the vocabulary for buying and selling at the marketplace.

One of the words used for buying a slave was also used for paying a ransom to free a hostage from captivity. After taking prisoners in battle, the victors allowed their freedom to be gained by the payment of a price called a *ransom*. This liberating process was called *redemption*. In Mark 10:45 Jesus identified His purpose in coming to earth with the word *ransom*: "The Son of man [came] . . . to give his life as a ransom for many." Because He knew who He was and why He came, He knew that His own life would be the purchase price to free slaves from sin's captivity.

Paul also used these terms borrowed from the worlds of commerce and warfare. He pictures Christ's transaction for us as freeing us from sin and its penalty and thus gaining our forgiveness from God. We "are justified freely by his grace through the redemption that came by Christ Jesus" (Romans 3:24). "In him we have redemption through his blood, the forgiveness of sins" (Ephesians 1:7; Colossians 1:14).

The central idea of "redemption" is to buy something by paying a price. That describes what Christ did for us. We were held captive, enslaved to sin, unable to free ourselves. Christ paid the purchase price, His own blood shed on the cross, to buy us out of the slave market of sin. First Peter 1:18-19 exposes the inability of the world's most valuable commodities, gold and silver, to purchase our redemption. Only Christ's death in our place could satisfy the requirements of God's righteousness and justice. The result is that we are no longer slaves to sin, and we are released from the court of God's justice.

To make sure that we don't misunderstand God's intent, Paul clarifies that our liberation from sin's slave market does not mean we're completely free—free to do anything we want. We are now owned by God. God is no longer our judge in the same sense that He was before our redemption, but He is our new Master. We are now His slaves as much as we were previously sin's slaves. "You are not your own; you were bought at a price" (1 Corinthians 6:19-20). That was a real and legal transaction. Paul's conclusion is simple and direct, "Therefore honor God with your body." Considering the price He paid to free us, it's not unreasonable for Him to demand that our lives be lived for His honor.

Back Together Again

Jesus' parable of the prodigal son ends with the father celebrating his son's return. Prior to this joyous reunion the relationship between father and son had been ruined by the son's rebellion. The father initiates a family party because reconciliation has occurred: "For this son of mine was dead and is alive again; he was lost and is found" (Luke 15:24).

The well-known prodigal story illustrates the reality between God and us. God made us for fellowship with Himself, but sin broke the relationship. The resulting enmity between us and God is so serious that Paul says "we were God's enemies" (Romans 5:10), "hostile to God" (Romans 8:7), and deserving His wrath (Romans 1:18; 5:9). A seemingly unbreachable barrier stands between us and God.

Reconciliation means a broken relationship with an offended person has been fixed. The basis for this renewed fellowship is that the offense that caused the hostility has been erased. Theologically, the alienation between us and God has been removed and the relationship restored. Because the barrier separating us from God has been taken away, we have peace with God (Romans 5:1).

We cannot remove the barrier of sin, but God does. He could not resolve this dilemma, however, by simply pronouncing the hostility over. His justice requires payment for our sin, which broke the relationship in the first place. But "God was reconciling the world to himself in Christ" (2 Corinthians 5:19). His substitutionary death was the means of reconciliation (Romans 5:10) as "God made him who had no sin to be sin for us" (2 Corinthians 5:21). God's pouring out His wrath on Christ, who was made sin for us, renders us savable. The shock is that God, the offended party, initiates and completes the reconciliation even while we are His enemies (Romans 5:10).

Christ's death achieves two additional reconciliations. The first is between Jews and Gentiles as depicted by Paul in Ephesians 2. The Old Testament ceremonial law led to ethnic and religious hostility between the two groups, but Christ "has made the two one and has destroyed the barrier, the dividing wall of hostility, by abolishing in his flesh the law with its commandments and regulations" (Ephesians 2:14-15). Second, He has accomplished God's plan "to bring all things in heaven and on earth together under one head, even Christ"

(Ephesians 1:10; Colossians 1:20). In God's proper timing this universal reconciliation will be fully implemented.

The gospel is the good news that God has removed the barrier that keeps us from Him. Paul says this ministry of reconciliation is entrusted to us (2 Corinthians 5:18-19). We verbally communicate the message when we speak the gospel to others, and we demonstrate its viability by living peacefully with one another. Christians should be passionate to show the gospel's truth in our treatment of others, especially other Christians. If we cannot exhibit a renewed relationship among one another, how would we expect the world to be interested in our message of reconciliation?

All in the Family

All people of compassion grieve over the neglect and abuse of unwanted or orphaned children. Fortunately, some of them are adopted by loving families. Just as human parents may adopt a child, God adopts us when we believe in Christ. "[T]o all who received him, to those who believed in his name, he gave the right to become children of God" (John 1:12). This does not mean, however, that we become equal with God's unique Son, Jesus. But as God's children, brothers and sisters of Christ and each other, and joint heirs with Jesus, we assume the privileges and obligations of God's family.

The Old Testament pictures God as a Father (Isaiah 43:6-7; 64:8; Malachi 1:6). The New Testament expands that image by saying God adopts us. In Galatians 4:1-7 Paul uses adoption to compare Old Testament believers' and New Testament believers' relationship with God. Israel's adoption was like an underage child, a servant, compared to the mature sonship of believers after Christ. And most shocking to Jews, God now includes Gentiles in His adoption plans (Galatians 3:26-29).

The background for adoption originates in the garden. God created Adam and Eve for a relationship with Himself, but their sin brought an end to that. God became an object of hostility to them and to us (Romans 8:7), and we all became "objects of wrath" (Ephesians 2:3) to Him. But on the cross, Christ took God's wrath for us. Now, if we drop our hostility to Him and receive Him by faith, God revives the relationship with us by adopting us as His children (Galatians 3:26).

As God's children we receive extraordinary benefits consistent with our new family relationship. For instance, we're freed from the law (Galatians 5:1), at least in the sense that the slave was obligated to it (Galatians 4:1-7). God provides for our needs in this life (Philippians 4:19). We enjoy divine guidance from the Spirit (Romans 8:14), and we become coheirs with Christ for eternity (Romans 8:17).

Our adoption process includes a yet future aspect. It won't be complete until we receive our resurrection bodies. "[W]e ourselves, who have the firstfruits of the Spirit, groan inwardly as we wait eagerly for our adoption as sons, the redemption of our bodies" (Romans 8:23). In the meantime the Spirit assures us of our status in God's family: "The Spirit himself testifies with our spirit that we are God's children" (Romans 8:16).

Like any father, our heavenly Father wants to ingrain His values and character within us (Ephesians 5:1). The process includes discipline, which is evidence of His love, "because the Lord disciplines those he loves, and he punishes everyone he accepts as a son" (Hebrews 12:6). Do you see evidence of God's "blood line" in your life? Does your relationship with your heavenly Father reflect the joy and responsibility of being His child? Does your treatment of your Christian siblings reflect the affection of God's family? Christians are God's children, and our lives should confirm our family ties.

Now What?

You lead someone to Christ, he turns to you and says, "Now what?" He believed, the game is over, and we won. Right? Some Christians think so. They believe Christianity is just getting people "saved." That's like saying we're physically born only to reproduce. But responsible parents make sure their children develop. If a child doesn't, they take her to the doctor to find out what's wrong because birth should lead to growth. The same is true spiritually. After birth comes growth—sanctification.

The Old Testament word for "sanctify" meant to set something aside for a special purpose and thus make it holy. The New Testament concept of being sanctified grows out of that Old Testament idea. The target of our sanctification is Christlikeness—a Spirit-produced change, freeing us from sinful habits and reforming us to the model of Christ. "For those God foreknew he also predestined to be conformed to the likeness of his Son" (Romans 8:29).

The Bible identifies three phases of sanctification:

positional, progressive, and ultimate. Positional sanctification is our new status in Christ (1 Corinthians 6:11; Hebrews 10:10,14). All believers are already sanctified in that sense. Progressive sanctification is the process of becoming like Christ now, after salvation and before death (2 Corinthians 3:18). That's the kind of sanctification most people talk about. Ultimate sanctification is complete Christlikeness and freedom from sin after we die and enter heaven (1 Corinthians 15:49; 1 John 3:2). All believers will eventually experience that.

Regeneration is the start—God's conceiving life in us. Glorification is the end—His destination for us. Sanctification is the middle—the route on which He leads us from start to finish. How does justification fit? Justification is God's legal statement that we're righteous in His sight, whereas sanctification is God's transforming work to make us righteous in character. The two are not identical, but God will finish what He starts. "[H]e who began a good work in you will carry it on to completion until the day of Christ Jesus" (Philippians 1:6).

The Spirit is the primary agent of sanctification (Romans 15:16; 1 Peter 1:2), and the Word is His principle tool. "Like newborn babies, crave pure spiritual milk, so that by it you may grow up in your salvation" (1 Peter 2:2). This corresponds to Paul's exhortation to "be transformed by the renewing of your mind" (Romans 12:2). The Bible offers no shortcuts to Christlikeness— we renew our minds by learning and living God's Word.

Sanctification is a divine, human cooperative effort. Consider Paul's deliberate balance in Philippians 2:12-13. "Continue to work out your salvation with fear and trembling, for it is God who works in you to will and to act according to his good purpose." The Spirit works in and through our God-dependent striving. Therefore, our role in sanctification is passive as we submit to the Spirit and trust Him to do His work, and active as we "press on to take hold of that for which Christ Jesus took hold of [us]" (Philippians 3:12).

Individual and corporate questions arise for self-examination: Are you more like Christ now than you were in the past? Are you practicing the historic disciplines of solitude, prayer, and meditation; reading and study of Scripture; witnessing, worship, and fellowship? Does your church grow Christians or just reproduce them?

Tell Me About the Guarantee

When we buy a product with a lifetime guarantee the salesperson says, "It's good forever, but keep it maintained or the warranty is voided." Is that a good analogy of salvation? Is it secure, or can we do something to void the warranty? The question introduces the overlapping doctrines of assurance and perseverance. Assurance is one's confidence of salvation regardless of an imperfect life. Perseverance is our steadfast belief and obedience to Christ, enduring to life's end.

The subject is often debated under the title "eternal security." The central question is, "Can Christians lose their salvation?" But perhaps the issue should be redirected: "Can unbelievers claim to be saved?" First John 2:19 answers the second question positively. "They went out from us, but they did not really belong to us. For if they had belonged to us, they would have remained with us; but their going showed that none of them belonged to us." Whatever the historical details, John says some professing Christians proved they were not genuine believers. They didn't lose salvation; they never had it in the first place. So, how does one know she is saved?

God sees the redemptive process as one continuous piece of work—His work. "For those God foreknew he also predestined to be conformed to the likeness of his Son. . . . And those he predestined, he also called; those he called, he also justified; those he justified, he also glorified" (Romans 8:29-30). Paul concludes that nothing can separate the true believer from God's love (Romans 8:38-39), and the Spirit Himself gives us a sense of assurance as He "testifies with our spirit that we are God's children" (Romans 8:16). His inner witness to us is part of what assures us that we are truly saved.

But mistaken assurance is common in a society which values religious respectability. Consider how many claim to be Christians by merely going to church or doing good deeds. Jesus, however, knows the false professors. "Many will say to me on that day, 'Lord, Lord, did we not prophesy in your name, and in your name drive out demons and perform many miracles?' Then I will tell them plainly, 'I never knew you'" (Matthew 7:22-23).

Jesus contended that "he who stands firm to the end will be saved" (Matthew 10:22; 24:13). Our need to persevere shouldn't scare us, because God preserves His own. Paul makes that point when writing the Philippians: "He who began a good work in you will carry it on to completion until the day of Christ Jesus" (Philippians 1:6). Jesus' death finished the work of redemption, and God sealed us by His Spirit (Ephesians 1:13; 4:30). The fulfillment of God's salvation project depends on His faithfulness, not our effort. The truly saved are secure in Christ.

Paul urges the wayward Corinthians, "Examine yourselves to see whether you are in the faith" (2 Corinthians 13:5). We prove our claim to faith is real by our life. Do you see some evidence of the indwelling Spirit in your life, such as the fruit of the Spirit (Galatians 5:22-23)? The presence of the fruit of the Spirit is some of the evidence we look for to verify our own salvation. We can rest in the Bible's assurance that God "is able to keep you from falling and to present you before his glorious presence without fault and with great joy" (Jude 24). Be assured that our failures (and we all have them) are temporary. God will keep His own forever. Unbelievers may claim to be saved when they're not, but the truly saved cannot lose their salvation.

God's Olive Wreath

The ancient Greek poet Pindar wrote glorious accolades about winners in the original Olympic games. Victors were crowned with an olive wreath, the greatest symbol of victory and glory in ancient Greece, comparable to Olympic gold today. As far as we know, none of those olive wreaths survive. Some of Pindar's odes do, but they too will vanish with time.

Pindar's glorification of ancient Olympians ranks among the greatest literature of antiquity. But it cannot compare to God's glorification of His saints, which will exceed any earthly honors. It will never fade or die, and it's already begun. As our sanctification proceeds we are even now "being transformed into [Christ's] likeness with ever-increasing glory" (2 Corinthians 3:18).

Paul lists glorification last in God's salvation process because it's not until Christ's return that we receive our resurrection bodies (Romans 8:28-30). Our present bodies are designed for life on earth, and Paul declares "that flesh and blood cannot inherit the kingdom of God" (1 Corinthians 15:50). But when Christ returns, our earthly bodies will be transformed into bodies like His, fit for heaven (Philippians 3:21). Our mortal, perishable, dishonorable bodies will become immortal, imperishable, and glorious, never victimized by sickness, disease, or death, or subject to sin.

Our moral and spiritual sanctification will also be complete when "death [is] swallowed up in victory" (1 Corinthians 15:53-54). Christ will present Himself with a "church, without stain or wrinkle or any other blemish . . . holy and blameless" (Ephesians 5:27). Our glorification will include vastly expanded knowledge. "Now I know in part; then I shall know fully, even as I am fully known" (1 Corinthians 13:12).

In our glorified state at the Final Judgment, we'll be fully vindicated of any charges. Our glorious, resurrection bodies will supply ample evidence of our justified status in God's eyes. "Since we have now been justified by his blood, how much more shall we be saved from God's wrath through him!" (Romans 5:9). Furthermore, we are coheirs with Christ and will share His glory, including reigning with Him forever (Romans 8:17; 2 Timothy 2:12). The effects of the Fall on the whole universe will also be reversed. Everything will be renewed, released from its condition of decay (Romans 8:19-21), including a new heaven, new earth, and new Jerusalem

(Revelation 21:1-2). Only such a place is fitting for glorified people.

The believer's hope is more than escape from judgment; it's eternal glory. We're encouraged by knowing that God is working toward our future glorification, the goal of His eternal plan for us. Because God will make us like His glorious Son in body and soul, the most discouraging times in this fallen world cannot diminish the hope of our future glory. Our spiritual struggles and failures will not continue forever. We will eventually be what God intends. God will be our eternal Pindar.

He, She, or It?

People speak freely of "the spirit" but they often mean an impersonal power, like the force in the *Star Wars* movies. That belief is increasingly common in the West as Eastern religions spread their teaching of pantheism—the idea that God and the impersonal universe are the same.

Denial of the Spirit's personality is not new. In the fourth century, Arius taught that the Spirit was only God's energy exerted into the world. Socinus taught a similar view in the sixteenth century—the Spirit was the energy proceeding from God. And today, Unitarians deny the Spirit's personality. Is the Spirit an impersonal "it" or a personal "who"?

The Bible argues that the Holy Spirit is a personal being, not an impersonal force. One argument comes from the pronouns used for the Holy Spirit. New Testament Greek nouns and pronouns have a trait called gender, which can be masculine, feminine, or neuter. The word for spirit, *pneuma*, is neuter. So, we would expect a neuter pronoun when used in place of

76 THE HOLY SPIRIT

249

pneuma. However, when *pneuma* refers to the Holy Spirit, the masculine pronoun appears, as in John 16:13: "When *he*, the Spirit of truth, comes, *he* will guide you into all truth" (emphasis added). John deliberately portrays the Holy Spirit as a personal being rather than an impersonal force.

A second argument for the Spirit's personality is the way the Spirit is associated with other persons, but distinguished from them. Matthew does this in 28:19 of his gospel: "baptizing them in the name of the Father and of the Son and of the Holy Spirit." Paul closes 2 Corinthians this way: "May the grace of the Lord Jesus Christ, and the love of God, and the fellowship of the Holy Spirit be with you all" (2 Corinthians 13:14). In other words, because the Spirit is associated with other persons, He is a person, but He is not just another name for the Father or the Son. Note how the Spirit is distinguished from the Father and the Son in John 14:26, "But the Counselor, the Holy Spirit, whom the Father will send in my name, will teach you all things and will remind you of everything I have said to you." Jesus is identifying the Holy Spirit as a personal being distinct from the Father and from Himself.

Another argument for the Spirit's personality is seen in the Spirit's activities, and the personal traits those activities imply. In John 16, for instance, the Spirit comforts, and guides, and teaches. Those activities all imply intelligence, will, and emotions—essential traits of personality not possessed by an impersonal force.

A final argument is found in verses where the Spirit is distinct from the generic power of God. In Acts 10:38 Peter says, "God anointed Jesus of Nazareth with the Holy Spirit and power." If the Holy Spirit is only God's impersonal power, Peter is speaking nonsense by repeating himself: "God anointed Jesus with power and with power."

The conclusion of these arguments can only be that the Holy Spirit is a person, not merely an impersonal force or a form of divine energy. Because the Spirit is a person, we can and should have a personal relationship with Him.

THE DEITY OF THE HOLY SPIRIT

Equal with the Father and the Son

The Spirit is the Person of the Godhead we deal with most directly. Understanding His nature is, therefore, essential for our Christian experience. We previously established that He is personal, but is He deity? The biblical evidence says yes—the Spirit is God in the same way and to the same degree as are the Father and the Son. Several arguments support this view.

First, the Spirit is directly called God. Peter's charge against Ananias in Acts 5:3-4 makes that connection. "Ananias . . . you have lied to the Holy Spirit . . . You have not lied to men but to God." Peter's view that lying to the Spirit was lying to God could not be true if the Spirit was not deity. Paul identifies the Spirit and the Lord interchangeably, making them equal: "Now the Lord is the Spirit" (2 Corinthians 3:17).

A second argument for the Spirit's deity arises from His possessing divine attributes. In Hebrews 9:14 He's described as "eternal." We find His omniscience in

1 Corinthians 2:11, "No one knows the thoughts of God except the Spirit of God." Psalm 139:7-8 reveals the Spirit's omnipresence, "Where can I go from your Spirit? . . . If I go up to the heavens, you are there; if I make my bed in the depths, you are there." Because the Spirit is pictured with traits only God possesses, He must be God.

The Spirit doing the works of God provides a third argument. For instance, John says the Spirit is the source of new birth, "No one can enter the kingdom of God unless he is born of water and the Spirit. Flesh gives birth to flesh, but the Spirit gives birth to spirit" (John 3:5-6). John then writes in 1 John 3:9 that Christians are "born of God." If God gives new birth, and the Spirit gives new birth, the Spirit must be God.

Finally, the Spirit is associated with the Father and the Son in a way that makes Him equal to both. Consider Paul's closing benediction of 2 Corinthians 13:14: "May the grace of the Lord Jesus Christ, and the love of God, and the fellowship of the Holy Spirit be with you all." Peter makes the same connection by referring to the elect as "chosen according to the foreknowledge of God the Father, through the sanctifying work of the Spirit, for obedience to Jesus Christ" (1 Peter 1:2). The Lord Himself implied the same equality by commanding us to "make disciples of all nations, baptizing them in the name of the Father and of the Son and of the Holy Spirit" (Matthew 28:19).

We conclude that the Holy Spirit is as divine as the Father and the Son. He is, therefore, worthy of equal respect, glory, and praise. We shouldn't demote Him to a lesser status than the Father or the Son any more than we would promote Him above them. Because of our ongoing intimate and permanent connection with the Spirit, the doctrine of His deity is as relevant as daily life. If He is divine, He can protect us, and provide for us without limit, and He will keep every promise He inspired in His Word.

Divine Ownership

In the ancient world, owners stamped their property with a private seal to verify legal possession. When kings or government officials drafted a formal document, they also sealed that record to certify the authority of what was written inside. The document was first rolled up like a scroll, then soft clay or hot wax was placed along the crease. The official then pressed his signet ring or a cylindrical seal onto the clay or wax, leaving an impression. That imprint carried the legal authority of a signature today, and anyone who broke the seal violated the authority of the one who sealed it.

Genesis 41:42 records an example of a ruler's signet ring. "Pharaoh took his signet ring from his finger and put it on Joseph's finger." King Darius of Persia sealed Daniel's den of lions with his signet ring as well as the signet rings of his officials (Daniel 6:17). A common business transaction—buying a field—was finalized by sealing the deed (Jeremiah 32:9-10). A man's personal seal was probably kept with him at all times and might be worn on a cord around his neck or arm (Genesis 38:18).

The practice of sealing is also found in the New Testament. The Roman troops sealed Jesus' tomb to secure it against theft (Matthew 27:66). Paul said the Corinthians were the authenticating seal of his apostleship (1 Corinthians 9:2).

That historical background forms the context for the sealing of the Holy Spirit. God seals each believer with His Spirit to secure us until the day of redemption when our salvation is complete. He stamps us with His official ownership by placing His seal, the Holy Spirit Himself, upon us. "Having believed, you were marked in him with a seal, the promised Holy Spirit, who is a deposit guaranteeing our inheritance until the redemption of those who are God's possession" (Ephesians 1:13-14). God's seal pictures the finished transaction of His purchasing us. It denotes His ownership and authority over us and our safety and security in Him. Paul says the inscription on God's seal reads, "The Lord knows those who are his" (2 Timothy 2:19).

This sealing occurs at salvation even though we don't sense it or experience it. Paul's wording in Ephesians 1:13-14 and 4:30 argues that every New Testament believer is sealed with the Spirit. Even the Corinthians, who were far from spiritually mature, were sealed. Paul includes them in writing that God "set his seal of ownership on us, and put his Spirit in our hearts as a deposit, guaranteeing what is to come" (2 Corinthians 1:22). Universal sealing is also assumed in Ephesians 4:30 because Paul exhorts all believers not to grieve the Holy Spirit with whom they were sealed.

Because God permanently sealed us with His Spirit, we are forever secure as His prized possession. No power on earth or in heaven, now or yet to come, is strong enough to break His seal upon us. Our final redemption rests entirely on God and His authority represented by His seal. No earthly discouragement or circumstance can change who owns and guards us. We are forever His, stamped with the seal of the Spirit, which no one can break.

Spiritual Immigration

Immigrants undergo a ceremony whereby they become citizens of this country. They don't experience any internal sensation, but their status changes. Their old citizenship in Thailand or Albania comes to an end, and they receive a new status, a new identity as Americans, including new rights and responsibilities. The "baptism of the Spirit" compares to that ceremonial transfer of status and identity.

The inception of Spirit baptism is the Acts 2 Pentecost event during which the Spirit came upon the believers there, all of whom were Jewish.

> Suddenly a sound like the blowing of a violent wind came from heaven and filled the whole house where they were sitting. They saw what seemed to be tongues of fire that separated and came to rest on each of them. All of them were filled with the Holy Spirit and began to speak in other tongues as the Spirit enabled them. (Acts 2:2-4)

After this cataclysmic event, the believers who had received the Spirit began to evangelize with power and passion, spreading the good news in many different languages. Similar incidents are recorded in Acts 8, 10, and 19.

Charismatic Christians associate Spirit baptism with speaking in "tongues" or other ecstatic experiences. They believe the baptism of the Spirit is an event that is separate from salvation, often occurring sometime after the believer has accepted Christ—but not to all believers. In this view, whether or not one has received this Spirit baptism is an indicator of a higher spiritual status.

The view presented here is that Spirit baptism and salvation occur simultaneously. The dramatic "tongues of fire" that touched the original Christians, and their miraculous ability to speak in other languages, were necessary to begin the spreading of the gospel, but they did not represent a compulsory standard for future Christians. In 1 Corinthians 12:13, Paul describes Spirit baptism as having already happened to the Corinthians, some of the most sinful, least "spiritual" Christians in the New Testament. The implication of Spirit baptism occurring at salvation is that all believers, not just an elite group, have received it.

Paul says the baptism of the Spirit is the Spirit's placing us into the body of Christ. "For we were all baptized by one Spirit into one body—whether Jews or Greeks, slave or free—and we were all given the one Spirit to drink" (1 Corinthians 12:13). Each new believer is thus identified with the universal church, Christ's body, of which He is the head (Colossians 1:18). This divine action transfers us into God's community.

The result is a new identity or citizenship—we're now "in Christ." We have a new status before God who sees us "in Christ" rather than "in Adam." "For as in Adam all die, so in Christ all will be made alive" (1 Corinthians 15:22). Even though we don't feel this transition, our Christian blessings flow from the new identity, our union with Christ. The recipients of the Spirit in the four incidents in Acts, mentioned above, did not seek it, nor does Scripture command us to do so. It is not a post-salvation second work of grace that we pursue, but part of God's once-and-for-all redemption package.

The Spirit's working in nonJewish believers provided compelling evidence for Peter and other Jewish Christian leaders that nonJews could become Christians. That may seem obvious to us, but the idea was new and startling to the infant Jewish church.

Because all believers are placed into the body of Christ, we have equal status before God regardless of race, sex, wealth, or giftedness. We are all spiritual immigrants transferred into His kingdom. The equality the world seeks is found only in God's miraculous uniting of all who come to Christ. In response, our treatment of one another should be as tender and caring as we give the parts of our own physical bodies (1 Corinthians 12:22-25).

A New Citizenship

If Spirit baptism compares to the ceremony for new citizens, "union with Christ" compares to the result—the citizenship itself. The baptism of the Spirit is an occurrence; union with Christ is a new status—our position or legal standing before God.

The concept of union with Christ could be discussed along with salvation because it occurs then, or with the Holy Spirit because He causes it. "For we were all baptized by one Spirit into one body" (1 Corinthians 12:13), and "all of you who were baptized into Christ have clothed yourselves with Christ" (Galatians 3:27). At salvation we become part of Christ's body, the universal church, of which He is the head, and every believer a member (Ephesians 4:15-16). Jesus Himself first introduced this new reality in John 14:20, "You are in me, and I am in you."

Jesus uses the relationship of the vine and the branches to depict the mutual indwelling of Christ and the believer: "Remain in me, and I will remain in you" (John 15:1-6). Paul's most common metaphor was the human body and its head. Christ is the "head over every-thing for the church, which is his body" (Ephesians 1:22-23). The marriage of husband and wife also illustrates the union of Christ and the church (Ephesians 5:23,32).

Our union with Christ is the basis for all our spiritual benefits. Because we are united with Him, we share in His crucifixion (Galatians 2:20), death (Romans 6:1-11), burial (Romans 6:4), resurrection (Colossians 3:1), life (Ephesians 2:5), ascension (Ephesians 2:6), reign (2 Timothy 2:12), inheritance, and glory (Romans 8:17). Everything Christ accomplished is credited to us.

Our old status included condemnation and death; our new status is a restored life, a fresh beginning. When the Father evaluates us, He no longer sees our flaws, weaknesses, and the evil in our hearts. He sees us exactly as He sees Christ, because we are one with Him. "Therefore, there is now no condemnation for those who are in Christ Jesus" (Romans 8:1). Consistent with our new status, we get a new nature which is being trans-formed into Christlikeness. "[Y]ou have taken off your old self with its practices and have put on the new self, which is being renewed in knowledge in the image of its Creator" (Colossians 3:9-10).

Our identification with Christ is not unlimited. First, it does not include a transfer of divine attributes. He forever remains fully divine; we never become deity in any way, at any time. Second, neither we nor Christ lose personal identity or distinctiveness. We don't merge into a single consciousness, but always stay personally separate from Him and from one another.

Newly converted Americans assume new duties when they accept their citizenship—they pledge to follow our laws and uphold our constitution. Christians also take on the responsibility of a new life—a holy life. We achieve increasing holiness because the power that raised Him from the dead now works in us (Romans 6). We "can do everything through him who gives [us] strength" (Philippians 4:13). By consistent trust in His power and obedience to His Word, we gain the spiritual high ground even in a fallen world.

God's House

Even when a car's engine is not running, it's still in the car—residual power waiting to spring into action. In a similar way, the Spirit's indwelling the believer's body forms the reservoir of our spiritual power. We don't always fully use that power source, but He's always there. His experiential control or influence over us may vary from time to time, but His indwelling is complete and permanent. Likewise, His indwelling and His baptism are distinct even though both occur at salvation.

Since Pentecost, the Spirit's indwelling is universal among Christians individually and collectively. "Don't you know that you yourselves are God's temple and that God's Spirit lives in you?" (1 Corinthians 3:16). We can logically conclude this universal indwelling from Romans 8:9, "If anyone does not have the Spirit of Christ, he does not belong to Christ." Jude announces the inescapable flipside—the unsaved "do not have the Spirit" (Jude 19). Our corporate indwelling is seen in Ephesians 2:22, "And in him you too are being built together to become a dwelling in which God lives by his Spirit."

Jesus promised that the Spirit would never leave us. "I will ask the Father, and he will give you another Counselor to be with you forever—the Spirit of truth" (John 14:16-17). Consequently, New Testament believers are never warned of the possible loss of the indwelling Spirit due to sin or other failures. Paul implies the opposite when he exhorts the sinning Corinthians to live a pure life because they are indwelt by the Spirit. "Do you not know that your body is a temple of the Holy Spirit, who is in you, whom you have received from God?" (1 Corinthians 6:19).

As part of salvation grace the Spirit's indwelling is a gift; we do not earn it. "God has poured out his love into our hearts by the Holy Spirit, whom he has given us" (Romans 5:5). The gift of the Spirit is a down payment that God will keep His other promises. "Now it is God who has . . . given us the Spirit as a deposit, guaranteeing what is to come" (2 Corinthians 5:5).

The Spirit did not permanently or universally indwell Old Testament believers, but entered and left individuals as He willed. "The Spirit came into" Ezekiel (Ezekiel 2:2; 3:24), implying that He had not been there before. Conversely, "the Spirit of the LORD . . . departed from Saul" (1 Samuel 16:14). That explains why, after David sinned with Bathsheba, he prayed, "Do not . . . take your

Holy Spirit from me" (Psalm 51:11).

The indwelling Spirit transmits His power to us (Acts 1:8) to the point that Jesus said we would do greater works than He did (John 14:12,16,17). As the temple of the Living God, our lives and our very bodies possess unique value. We are God's house. One observable consequence of the Spirit's indwelling is the unity He brings to the church (Acts 4:32). Our care and concern for the well-being of the body of Christ can surpass our focus on ourselves and our interests. That unity provides a powerful argument for the truth of Christianity. Every believer and every church should consider if their unity presents a strong case for the faith.

Supernatural Power

Police charge drunk drivers with "driving under the influence" because alcohol influences judgment, decisions, and actions. Surprisingly, Paul compares being drunk with being Spirit-filled. "Do not get drunk on wine, which leads to debauchery. Instead, be filled with the Spirit" (Ephesians 5:18). From that analogy, we can see that both alcohol and the Spirit can wield control over us if we let them.

Being Spirit-filled is not our getting more of the Spirit, but His getting more of us. The Spirit already indwells each believer, but residence alone does not imply control. The Galatians possessed the Spirit from the time of salvation, but Paul had to chastise them for pursuing the Christian life by their own effort instead of by the Spirit. "After beginning with the Spirit, are you now trying to attain your goal by human effort?" (Galatians 3:3). They were not allowing the indwelling Spirit to influence them, at least not much.

Our cooperation with the Spirit is a joint effort. We cooperate with Him so He can do His part in us as we do ours. Note the mix of Spirit filling and human responsibility in Acts 6:3: "Brothers, choose seven men from among you who are known to be full of the Spirit and wisdom. We will turn this responsibility over to them." Our cooperating with the Spirit allows Him to do what He wills in and through us. He could force us to do what He wants, but He does not do everything He could do. His control does not negate our mental, volitional, and physical capacities.

Because the Ephesians 5:18 command is present tense, we're to be repeatedly or continually filled. This repeated filling is needed because we can reduce or remove it. Even under the Spirit's influence, we retain our ability to choose, including to choose sin, and thus we can diminish the Spirit's filling. Conversely, even in sin, we can surrender to the Spirit's control again. Much of the time we oscillate between the two influences of our sinful nature and the Holy Spirit (Romans 7).

The means of Spirit filling is not a tidy one-two-three list. But Scripture does give us clues for how to stay filled with the Spirit: Resist temptation and submit to the Spirit (Romans 12:1); depend on His power for living (Galatians 2:20); obey His commands (1 John 2:6). When we do sin, confess it (1 John 1:9). Otherwise we grieve the Spirit (Ephesians. 4:30), and when we resist Him we stifle His influence (1 Thessalonians 5:19).

The Spirit's filling heightens our awareness of His inner presence and increases the effectiveness of our spiritual gifts. When we're filled with the Spirit, we desire to do what He wants and the fruit of the Spirit grows in our soul. We maximize His control by letting Him be the dominant influence on our thoughts, words, and deeds. As redeemed people living in a fallen world, we must depend on the Spirit to help us live as God wants us to. God says His work is done "not by might nor by power, but by my Spirit" (Zechariah 4:6). "Since we live by the Spirit, let us keep in step with the Spirit" (Galatians 5:25). Because of this, our own shortcomings need not hinder our usefulness in God's hands.

The Spirit's Player Draft

NFL teams draft football players to build the right mix for their club's success. They need different kinds of athletes to fill the team's diverse positions. A roster of all quarterbacks but no lineman or running backs or receivers would fail miserably. They reach their goal by finding and using players with different abilities.

The Holy Spirit builds God's team, the church. It operates best with different players in the right positions, called spiritual gifts, special abilities believers use in serving the body of Christ. Every believer has at least one, because the Spirit "gives them to each one, just as he determines" (1 Corinthians 12:11). God provided all the positions on the team, and He blends our gifts in a way that builds the church and elevates our need of one another. He wants every believer active in ministry. "Now you are the body of Christ, and each one of you is a part of it" (1 Corinthians 12:27). Consequently, all the gifts are essential.

The Bible records several lists of spiritual gifts (Romans 12:6-8; 1 Corinthians 12:8-10,28; Ephesians

83 | THE HOLY SPIRIT

4:11), and they can be grouped into two broad categories, speaking gifts and serving gifts. Neither set is superior to the other. Whether in the spotlight or the shadows, faithful use is what counts: "Each one should use whatever gift he has received to serve others, faithfully administering God's grace in its various forms" (1 Peter 4:10).

One example of a speaking gift is teaching (Romans 12:7; 1 Corinthians 12:28-29). The teacher studies and explains God's truth to God's people to renew their minds and transform their lives (Romans 12:2). Paul's connection of the teaching gift with being a pastor (Ephesians 4:11) tells us that a pastor who doesn't teach is not fully doing his job. Mercy is an example of a serving gift (Romans 12:8). Someone with this gift quickly sees those in need and knows what to do. He or she cheerfully and naturally (supernaturally!) comforts the sick, the depressed, the downtrodden.

Two of the more spectacular gifts mentioned in the Bible are prophecy and speaking in tongues. These gifts are the focal point for a controversy that exists in the church today over whether God intended all the gifts to be permanent until Christ returns, or some gifts to be temporary to help establish the infant church. Most charismatics believe God intended all the gifts to be permanent, and hence they expect a certain number of believers to have the gifts of prophecy or tongues. Noncharismatics believe He designed those two gifts specifically to assist the early believers in spreading the gospel, but those gifts were no longer to be granted once Scripture had been recorded, or at the end of the apostolic age, or a similar termination point. In this view, we would not look for contemporary believers with the gifts of prophecy or tongues.

Either way, the purpose of spiritual gifts is anothers' benefit, not self-glory or personal fulfillment. Paul highlights that divine intent in 1 Corinthians 12:7; "Now to each one the manifestation of the Spirit is given for the common good." God holds us responsible to humbly use our gift(s) for the maturing of the body "as each part does its work" (Ephesians 4:16).

If we neglect our gift(s) we fall short of our God-given potential. We also rob the church of what God gave us for it. Since our individual spiritual growth is tied to the whole body, we also cheat ourselves as well. As we use the gift(s) God gave us, His team prospers and He is glorified.

Divine Production

Different trees may look alike until they bear fruit. Then we can distinguish between apple, orange, and walnut trees. The same with people. They may seem similar until they bear fruit, revealing internal character. Even Christians fall into this false means of appraising people externally by elevating spiritual gifts above all else. But a careful reading of 1 Corinthians 12-14 reveals Paul's intent of taming the Corinthians' wild passion for spiritual gifts. They glorified the gifts of the Spirit to the neglect of more important things, like the fruit of the Spirit—the character traits of Christlikeness. Paul believed that spiritual fruit, not his gifts, reveals a Spirit-controlled life. The benefit of even the most spectacular gifts is lost without love (1 Corinthians 13:1-3).

"The fruit of the Spirit" is Paul's metaphor for character traits of people controlled by the Spirit: "love, joy, peace, patience, kindness, goodness, faithfulness, gentleness and self-control" (Galatians 5:22-23). He may have borrowed the fruit metaphor from the Old Testament, which compares Israel to "a fruitful vineyard"

(Isaiah 27:2-6). It may also be significant that love, which heads Paul's list of the fruit of the Spirit (Galatians 5:22), fulfills the Ten Commandments: "He who loves his fellowman has fulfilled the law. The commandments . . . are summed up in this one rule: 'Love your neighbor as yourself.' Love does no harm to its neighbor. Therefore, love is the fulfillment of the law" (Romans 13:8-10).

The Galatian believers were returning to the Mosaic Law in a way that Paul interpreted as a retreat from the gospel of grace. He strongly urged them to live by the Spirit instead. "If you are led by the Spirit, you are not under law" (Galatians 5:18). He also exhorted them to avoid the opposite extreme, the appeal of the flesh, by means of the Spirit. "So I say, live by the Spirit, and you will not gratify the desires of the sinful nature" (Galatians 5:16). Neither the Law of Moses nor the works of man can produce the fruit of the Spirit (Galatians 5:22-23).

Paul identifies the fruit of the Spirit with three sets of three traits. The first includes love—the selfless attitude that acts on behalf of others' needs; joy—a deep, inner happiness despite the outer circumstances of life; and peace—a tranquil spirit. The second set is comprised of patience—steadfast fortitude under life's pressures; kindness—love in action; and goodness—moral excellence. The third set includes faithfulness—our reliability or trustworthiness; gentleness—strength held in reserve; and self-control—mastery of our passions. The Christian life is more than avoiding negatives; it manifests positive traits—the fruit of the Spirit which describes the character and lifestyle God intends for His people.

Such traits are not the result of quick-fix decisions or emotional experiences, but the result of long-term transformation of soul. Holiness is not found in easy or simple cure-alls. The goal of this spiritual fruit surpasses individual character formation. It benefits the church, God's community on earth. Its consistent presence in the church gives evidence of the Spirit's presence and a foretaste of heaven.

God's Group

Some Christians, especially in the Western world, possess a Lone Ranger attitude toward Christianity: "Jesus and me are all I need." We may be saved by individual faith, but God includes millions in His salvation plan. This corporate element introduces the church.

The original word "church" carried no religious or spiritual meaning. It was used in the ancient Greek world for any group called together for a meeting. Its most common biblical use is for the group of people who believed in Christ.

Sometimes it spoke of Christians who met in one place: "To the church of God in Corinth" (1 Corinthians 1:2). Other times it was used for all Christians everywhere through all time as in Colossians 1:18, "And He [Christ] is the head of the body, the church." The first meaning is called the local church; the second, the universal church. It never meant a building or a denomination such as Baptist or Presbyterian church. Church buildings did not exist until the third century, and denominations did not exist for centuries after that.

85 THE CHURCH

277

Jesus said He would build His church (Matthew 16:18). So, a simple definition of the church is all the people Jesus calls to Himself. But who are they? We cannot know for sure because, in one sense, the church is invisible. We cannot see the condition of a person's heart to know if he or she is a genuine believer. But in a different sense, the church is visible. We can see those who claim to be Christians, and, by the way they live, give some evidence of genuine faith. This distinction between the invisible and visible church implies that unbelievers may be found within local churches. This is especially true in countries with a Christian heritage, like America, where people often consider themselves Christians without knowing what that means.

What distinguishes a true from a false church? First, the group must at least claim to be Christians. Any group that says they are not believers, obviously, is not a church. Second, they must believe and preach Christian teaching, found in the Bible. If a group claims to be Christian, but rejects the Bible, this is not a true church, in the same way that someone who rejects the teachings of Karl Marx cannot rightly claim to be a Marxist. Finally, the group must intend to be a church. Many Christian groups, such as Christian colleges and home Bible studies, do not claim to be a church or intend to become a church. The biblical sign of this intent is the practice of the sacraments—special "rituals" in which we experience and celebrate God's presence, learn to be receptive to Him, and draw closer to Him. Most Protestant churches recognize baptism and communion (the Lord's Supper) as the only sacraments, although Roman Catholic and Orthodox churches include others such as marriage, confession, and confirmation.

So, functionally, a church is a group of Christians, who believe and proclaim the Bible, and intend to function as a church. No church is perfect, but if it meets the three functional aspects noted above, God can use us in it and through it to those on the outside.

Why Does the Church Exist?

A weight lifter who works only arms or legs doesn't develop physical symmetry. He becomes lopsided, in extreme cases a grotesque distortion. In a similar way a church that pursues only one purpose and neglects others mutates into something God never planned. Those imbalanced churches produce spiritually lopsided people.

What is the church's purpose? We must first recognize that God did, in fact, design the church for a purpose. He never intended a religious bureaucracy that exists only to perpetuate itself. Jesus' people were left on earth to fulfill His mission, and when churches lose that sense of direction, it shows. God's purpose for the church can be expressed as a responsibility in four areas: God, the lost, the saved, and the needy.

Responsibility toward God: First and foremost, the church's purpose is worship. He chose us "for the praise of his glory" (Ephesians 1:11-12). What we often call worship—congregational singing—sets the tone for the proclamation of the Word, but worship is also an end in itself. Acknowledging the worth of the One who redeemed us is no mere warm-up to "the real thing." Worship is also a moment-by-moment reality, a continual attitude, a life of being Christlike, obeying His Word. If we don't worship, we miss the glorious sensation God planned for His praise and our joy.

Responsibility toward the lost: Jesus spoke of the mission to the lost long before He gave the Great Commission in Matthew 28:19-20. Early in His ministry, He informed His disciples that He would redirect the target of their fishing from fish to men (Luke 5:1-11). He later told them to bring in the spiritual harvest (Matthew 9:37-38). Jesus' mission of evangelism is not optional for His followers. Individually and corporately, we're to be intentional in seeking the lost with God's good news of grace in Christ.

Responsibility toward the saved: The church's purpose also includes the found. The Great Commission calls us to "make disciples," that is learners, apprentices of Jesus. Churches who emphasize evangelism but neglect spiritual growth have stopped at step one—spiritual birth, when there's a lifetime of learning and living to follow. Paul was consumed with presenting everyone perfect or mature in Christ (Colossians 1:28), and God gave spiritual gifts to grow the saints (Ephesians 4:12-13) "until Christ is formed in you" (Galatians 4:19).

Responsibility toward the needy: The church's mandate is to love the needy, do good to them, and be merciful to them (Luke 6:35-36). Some churches turn inward, seeing only the needs of their own, blind to the lives of those outside. They miss the opportunity to display in a concrete way the reconciliation with God offered by Christ. Barriers of race and social status can be removed, at least in part, as we bring Christ's healing grace to the turmoil of human tensions. Social engagement never replaces evangelism but walks hand in hand with sharing the good news of God's mercy.

Churches should blend these multiple purposes into a seamless whole rather than allow them to compete with one another. A healthy church will not be so captivated by one purpose that it neglects the others. Our mix of spiritual gifts should result in an integrated church life of evangelism, edification, worship, and social impact, all to the glory of God. Let's not present to the world a lopsided, grotesque caricature of God's church.

Why So Many Churches?

Observers of Christianity ask, "Why are there are so many denominations?" One would think that if Christians believe more or less the same basic teachings, they would have just one church. Indeed Paul expressed this ideal to the dividing church in Corinth, "I appeal to you, brothers, in the name of our Lord Jesus Christ, that all of you agree with one another so that there may be no divisions among you and that you may be perfectly united in mind and thought" (1 Corinthians 1:10). But current observation and church history reveal the opposite.

The biblical basis for unity among Christians starts with Jesus' prayer for His followers: "that all of them may be one, Father, just as you are in me and I am in you" (John 17:21). The early church fathers tried to preserve that unity by focusing Christians on the apostles' gospel and teaching. Unity was largely maintained by church councils called together to discuss doctrinal differences and oppose outright heresy.

Other than a few minor divisions, the church remained one for its initial thousand years. The first major split came in 1054 when the Eastern church, centered in Constantinople, separated from the Western church, based in Rome, over the pope's adding a phrase to the Nicene Creed. The dividing issue was not just doctrine, but who possessed authority to change it. The Western church split further into Roman Catholic and various Protestant groups during the sixteenth century Reformation. Most of the divisions were over which doctrines to emphasize, and where the authority for deciding doctrine was found. Some nonRoman groups tried to remain within the Roman Catholic Church but were excommunicated. Other, more radical groups separated from everyone, even other Protestants. Over the next centuries, Protestantism continued to divide into hundreds of subgroups.

In the nineteenth century, some Christians grew dissatisfied with the growing number of denominations. American Christians from a broad range of denominations began cooperating in missions work and Bible societies. The modern ecumenical movement (an effort to bring some unity to the many denominations) began in 1910 at a missionary conference in Edinburgh, Scotland, leading to the formation of the World Council of Churches (WCC) in 1948.

Roman Catholics and evangelicals usually have not

joined ecumenical efforts. Catholics remain separate for doctrinal reasons and their claim of the pope's authority. Evangelicals have doctrinal and sometimes political reasons to remain separate, not wanting to be involved with the WCC's apparent politically left agenda. To preserve historic doctrine and promote the gospel, many evangelicals have aligned among themselves in groups such as the National Association of Evangelicals (NAE). So today, the WCC-affiliated churches tend to be more liberal, and the more conservative churches can be found among the NAE.

Denominational names no longer mean as much as they used to. Being a Lutheran, Presbyterian, or Methodist might mean almost anything along the doctrinal continuum. The historic name tag says little about a church's theology, style of worship, or ministry emphasis. Many Christians find the movement away from denominationalism a refreshing return to a more biblically centered Christianity.

Who's at the Controls?

One of life's most vexing problems is government. We take it for granted but someone must be at the steering wheel of society. How do we organize and lead the complex factors that order human life? Throughout history, cultures and countries have experimented with tyrannies, monarchies, oligarchies, republics, and democracies, resulting in varying degrees of success.

The church is not immune from this task. Predictably, Christians argue over forms of government, although it's not a core doctrine of the faith. Nevertheless, concerns over leadership, authority, and organization cannot be ignored. While Scripture offers no clear decree, detectable principles and patterns can guide us today.

Built on the foundation of Jesus Christ (1 Corinthians 3:11), the church began under the oversight of His apostles. The general sense of *apostle* is "messenger" (Philippians 2:25), but it's applied to the men Christ commissioned to write Scripture and establish His church (Ephesians 2:20). Because the qualifications for apostleship are no longer possible—having seen the resurrected

Christ (Acts 1:22) and being directly commissioned by Him (Matthew 10:1-7)—there are no apostles today.

The early church chose other men to help the twelve with the physical needs, allowing the apostles to focus on the Word and prayer (Acts 6:2-4). Though "deacon" does not appear in the passage, the function of the seven chosen to help the apostles is the same as today's deacons. The word means "servant," often helping with material and financial needs.

Because the apostles would eventually die, "elders" were appointed to lead and teach local churches (Acts 14:23; 1 Timothy 5:17). When the apostles traveled and when they eventually died, elders assumed local church leadership. They led and taught, including some who devoted enough time to study and teaching that Paul said they should be paid (1 Timothy 5:17).

In Ephesians 4:11 Paul mentions "pastors and teachers," but the word should probably be translated as one gift, "pastor-teachers." Pastor is from the word "shepherd," whose job is to take care of or feed the flock (John 21:16). The key pastoral role of feeding the flock is accomplished by furnishing the spiritual food of God's Word.

Three forms of church government emerged from the Reformation.

Episcopal government: The most structured form of

church leadership is the episcopal, which includes multiple levels of bishops in whom, it is thought, the power of God resides.

Presbyterian government: Centering around the office of presbyter or elder, the Presbyterian style of government looks on the elders as the highest (human) church authority. Elders are chosen by God and confirmed by the people. Even at the Jerusalem Council of Acts 15 (about A.D. 50) elders were functioning under the apostles.

Congregational government: This third form of government emphasizes the individuals in the church, as in a political democracy. Most decisions are determined by a vote of the people. These self-governing local churches are under no jurisdiction from outside authority.

Because the Bible does not prescribe one form of church government, we cannot say any modern form is God's exact model. But it appears that some type of elder leadership most closely corresponds to the early church pattern. A spiritually sensitive church with qualified leaders and motivated people make any form of church government workable. If we seek the Spirit as we learn and obey His Word, He will use us regardless of our structure.

No Sin, Heresy, Hostility, or Division

Basketball teams need talent and teamwork. Great athletes wracked by dissension often lose because the infighting neutralizes the skills that bring victory. Teams with lesser ballplayers but unified commitment are usually successful. That collective passion elevates their game to another dimension and applies it to the task at hand.

This analogy may compare to purity and unity in the church. A church without sin and heresy reflects purity; its avoidance of hostility and division reveals unity. Both sides are needed, but they tend to work in opposite directions. Striving for perfect purity might exclude people deemed less pure such as those holding a minor deviation on some small doctrinal point. Likewise, seeking complete unity might compromise purity by tolerating members in flagrant, persistent sin. We should note that the point applies only to church members, not seekers.

Purity and unity are balanced only by the indwelling Spirit. We can be pure because the Spirit of the Holy One

89 | THE CHURCH

resides within us individually and corporately. "Do you not know that your body is a temple of the Holy Spirit, who is in you, whom you have received from God?" (1 Corinthians 6:19). We can find unity because the Spirit merges us in Christ. "For we were all baptized by one Spirit into one body—whether Jews or Greeks, slave or free—and we were all given the one Spirit to drink" (1 Corinthians 12:13).

No church is completely pure. And purity is not one broad category but a complex array of diverse factors: intimacy with God, avoidance of sin, sound doctrine, compelling preaching and teaching, vibrant worship, loving fellowship, fervent evangelism, and compassionate social involvement. What church rates an A on all those? Nevertheless, Paul labored to present the church as a pure virgin to Christ (2 Corinthians 11:2). The process continues today—we're all to work at building the church (1 Corinthians 14:12). The path is long and hard and often frustrating but Christ assigned the task to us.

The Lord Himself calls us to unity. "May they be brought to complete unity to let the world know that you sent me and have loved them even as you have loved me" (John 17:23). Conversely, Paul sternly warns of divisiveness. "Warn a divisive person once, and then warn him a second time. After that, have nothing to do with him"

(Titus 3:10). But unity means many things to different people. It can be viewed as merely spiritual—all believers are united in Christ. Some people value an active alliance in which differing Christians can work together for common goals. Others see unity as denying our differences and merging all churches into one. Because Christian unity must be based on being "in Christ," total organizational unity, including groups that deny Christ, is beyond biblical bounds. Such "unity" destroys purity.

All Christians should ask questions about their church. How pure and united is it? How can we improve each? What would my church look like if I took steps to elevate its purity? Its unity? How do we integrate the two? While we strive to do what we can, the Spirit is the one who gives purity and unity. As we grow together toward Christlikeness, our purity and our unity will increase and honor Him.

A Sign of Love

A mother who does not discipline her child for playing in the street is not acting in love. Children need training and correction to survive the dangers of childhood and grow up well. Loving parents know that, and chasten their children for their own good. God does the same with His children, "because the Lord disciplines those he loves, and he punishes everyone he accepts as a son" (Hebrews 12:6). His loving correction, including punishment, proves that we really are His children. He sometimes disciplines us directly, but He also delegates the responsibility of discipline to His family, the church (Matthew 18:15-17).

The word "discipline" includes a positive side, instruction, as well as a negative side, punishment. Churches that neglect either do not provide an environment for spiritual growth. Believers develop, in part, by the suffering that comes through discipline. Churches must hold their members accountable as many New Testament examples show (1 Corinthians 5:1-13; 2 Corinthians 2:5-11; 2 Thessalonians 3:6,14-15; Titus 1:10-14; 3:9-11).

90

THE CHURCH

The policy and practice of church discipline becomes more important when the church increasingly reflects the values of the surrounding society more than it does God's Word.

Some churches no longer believe in or apply discipline. And among those who do, some sins are considered more worthy of discipline than others. A "big" sin such as adultery is a more likely candidate for discipline than "lesser" sins. But the Bible avoids that division. Paul's list of sins in Galatians 5:19-21 includes jealousy, selfish ambition, and dissensions along with sexual immorality, idolatry, and drunkenness. Perhaps a better distinction is found between persistent, public sins that damage the body in a major way, and those that are less frequent and visibly destructive. After all, does anything harm the church more than long-term gossip and divisiveness? Does God tolerate verbally destroying the body more than He does other sins?

The intent of church discipline is not vengeance or just plain meanness but repentance and restoration of God's sinning child. A believer in sin needs to be awakened to his own spiritual danger and to the damage done to the body. The church's public credibility and internal integrity are preserved as sin and heresy are addressed and removed.

Based on Jesus' teaching in Matthew 18:15-17 and Paul's application in 1 Corinthians 5:3-13, Galatians 6:1, and Titus 3:10, the discipline procedure includes three steps. First, private confrontation. If repentance is not forthcoming, a second encounter with a witness or church leader. Then, if the sinning member still refuses to repent, announcement to the whole church. If repentance never occurs, expulsion follows. If, however, the offending party repents anywhere in the process, the church should restore him to fellowship (2 Corinthians 2:6-8).

As with many issues, the church must avoid extremes. One is ducking its responsibility of discipline because an over-tolerant society frowns on any restraint. The other is forgetting grace and mercy because some zealots want to discipline every possible offense. The application of discipline is neither fun nor easy, but is required to protect the body. With wise and gracious strength, God's people must maintain and protect the church, and love its own sinners enough to call them back from sin.

Ultimate Honor

Our cultural idols are money, success, power, pleasure, and ourselves. Their enticements draw us toward themselves and away from God—the only rightful object of worship. Since whatever we worship influences us, we become like our idols, increasingly adopting and reflecting their traits. God had that in mind when He created us to worship Him—that we become more and more like Him as we adore Him more and more.

Worship is an attitude before it becomes an action. Our word "worship" speaks of the "worthship" of the one being revered. In our fallen state, we're able to treat people or things like gods, but He won't share His glory (Isaiah 48:11; Exodus 20:5). Thus He started the Ten Commandments: "You shall have no other gods before me" (Exodus 20:3-4).

Because God made us for His glory, worship is our highest calling (Isaiah 43:7). Nothing in life deserves the honor due Him, and heaven's cry will forever be, "You are worthy, our Lord and God, to receive glory and honor and power" (Revelation 4:11). In His timelessness, He

91 THE CHURCH

295

continually receives all the worship ever given Him through the ages. He will eternally enjoy every song we sing, every prayer we utter, every cry of our heart, as they are always before Him.

We may think worship is an activity in a certain building on one day of the week. But ancient Israel incorporated worship into daily life, especially keeping God's Law always before their eyes (Deuteronomy 6:7). Because the early church came from a Jewish heritage, it retained that view of worship as a way of life. The New Testament doesn't record the details of early church services, but they appear simple, centering on the Word, prayer, fellowship, and the Lord's Supper (Acts 2:42). Over the centuries, the inner adoration of God was replaced by external ritual—the people watching a priest perform at an altar. But after the Reformation, many churches changed their worship format to include participation by the people.

Because the Bible does not prescribe worship order, churches are free to design services to enhance the worship experience fitting for each culture. But several components are found in the New Testament. On his prison deathbed Paul commanded Timothy—"Preach the Word" (2 Timothy 4:2). Paul tells the Thessalonian church to "pray continually" (1 Thessalonians 5:17). He assumed the Colossian Christians sang psalms, hymns, and spiritual songs to God (Colossians 3:16). In 1 Corinthians 11, he reiterates the practice of the Lord's Supper.

Despite variations of corporate worship tradition, all churches should consider the same guiding principles—don't violate Scripture, be guided by the Spirit, and focus on God alone. For deepest worship to occur, our minds, emotions, and wills must be fully committed to the experience, consumed by God and His glory. Activities that have stagnated into stale rituals should be reconsidered. Are they really worship? Do our patterns and practices truly worship God or reinforce our nostalgia? God, not tradition, must guide our worship.

Christian Initiation

New members of a social club undergo an initiation including embarrassing or humiliating treatment. The intent is to have some laughs at the initiate's expense. But the more serious purpose is to demonstrate the person's identity with the group, even though they were formally accepted at a previous time. The public initiation symbolizes that prior admission.

Baptism is similar to initiation. Our English word "baptize" comes from the Greek verb *baptizo*, "to dip, plunge, immerse." But its ancient usage suggests a more fundamental sense of association between the thing immersed and what it's placed into. The common use became a religious rite of cleansing and identification. In our context, it is the public sign of alliance with Jesus Christ.

This simple yet significant act has been practiced from the beginning of the church (Acts 2:41), but the rite of baptism did not begin with Christianity. Ancient Jews ritually washed their priests, their sacred instruments, and converts to Judaism (Leviticus 8:6; Mark 7:3-4).

John the Baptist baptized people as a sign of repentance to prepare for the coming kingdom (Matthew 3:1-2,6). Jesus was baptized to identify with His messianic mission (Matthew 3:13-15).

Both the meaning and the method of Christian baptism is debated. Doctrinal differences usually center on "sprinkling versus immersion" and "baptism at birth versus baptism after salvation."

Some Christians believe baptism is a sign of being part of God's covenant community, similar to circumcision in the Old Testament. Thus they baptize infants by pouring or sprinkling. Other Christians take the position that baptism symbolizes the Christian's identification with Christ in His death, burial, and resurrection, dying to the old life of sin and rising to new life in Christ (Romans 6:4,11). In this case, individuals are baptized only after they have made a conscious decision to accept Christ as their Savior—the experience of salvation. Water baptism is the outer portrayal of the inner baptism of the Spirit, by which the Spirit placed the believer in union with Christ at the time of salvation.

Because baptism is a symbol, the method is less essential than what the symbol represents. Nevertheless, the word implies immersion. Different methods offer more or less accurate images of the meaning of baptism.

While pouring or sprinkling can be understood to symbolize death, burial, and resurrection, they don't mirror that reality as closely as immersion does—going under and coming out of the water.

Some Christians believe infants were included in the household baptisms of Acts 16:15, 16:33, and 1 Corinthians 1:16. The alternate view is that this claim goes beyond the biblical evidence—every reported baptism is for someone who already expressed faith in Christ. Furthermore, in this view, if baptism symbolizes initial union with Christ and the entrance into the Christian life, it shouldn't be administered to someone who has not yet consciously believed in Christ.

All Christians should be baptized because Jesus commanded us to baptize Christ's disciples (Matthew 28:19-20). Doing so reviews the gospel message for all who watch, and reminds the one being baptized of the new life to live. Baptism is our public initiation that tells others we have been accepted into God's group—the body of Christ.

Bittersweet Memories

Memories can be both joyous and sad. We recall glorious times with loved ones, but yearn for their return while we're apart. Memories sustain us during the absence, and make us long for their presence. The Lord's Supper does the same—we recall what He did for us and look for His return. We remember His death and anticipate His coming back (Matthew 26:26-29; Mark 14:22-25; Luke 22:19-20; 1 Corinthians 11:24-26). The Lord's Supper is variously referred to as Communion or the Eucharist.

Jesus' actions and words are set against the back-drop of the Jewish Passover. On His last night with His disciples, Jesus broke the bread and drank the wine, saying, "Do this in remembrance of me." He intended us to see Him as our Passover Lamb, slain to free us from sin and death, as the Exodus generation was freed from Egyptian bondage.

The nature of the Lord's Supper is understood differently by various Christian traditions. All agree that Jesus commands us to remember Him by ceremonially

93 THE CHURCH

breaking bread and drinking wine; hence all Christian churches include the Lord's Supper as a regular sacrament. The disagreement occurs over what actually happens with the bread and the wine. The Roman Catholic Church teaches "transubstantiation," which says the bread and wine are literally transformed into the body and blood of Christ. Luther rejected that view for what was later called "consubstantiation," which understands Christ's body and blood as mysteriously present in the bread and wine. The Calvinist or Reformed idea is that the bread and wine are not changed into Christ's body and blood, but are spiritually contained within them. Many other Protestant positions deny the literal presence of Christ in the bread and wine, seeing them as purely symbolic—a memorial of Christ's death.

The Lord's Supper symbolizes Christ's sacrificial death for us, satisfying the Father's wrath against sin. "For whenever you eat this bread and drink this cup, you proclaim the Lord's death until he comes" (1 Corinthians 11:26). Specifically, the bread and the cup picture Christ's broken body and shed blood on our behalf. Communion also conveys hope for the future as it anticipates His return, found in the phrase, "until He comes." Our unity as one body appears in 1 Corinthians 10:17, "Because there is one loaf, we, who are many, are one body, for we all partake of the one loaf." When we partake of the elements we restate our commitment to Him, to love one another in unity, and to serve others in the body and the world as He served us.

During those minutes of Communion, we should fully concentrate our minds and hearts on Him and His death. The Lord's Supper acts as a test, an internal private exam, to see how well we can focus on the Lord of Glory and the price He paid for us. If we cannot concentrate on Him for that short time, it may reveal our lack of passion for Him and our ingratitude for what He did. As we spiritually grow more like Him, we're able to hold Him in the center of our thoughts more and more, not only during Communion but throughout each day. The Lord's Supper can be a testing center for our ongoing intimacy with Him who died to set us free.

The End of the Line

Humanity faces a universal dilemma—we will all die! Regardless of race, culture, or religion, every person knows the outcome of this life—death. Whatever we may think we can do to delay, avoid, or ignore it, the end will come for each of us. The issue is so fundamental that every religion addresses the termination of life, and Christianity is no different.

In the Bible, human life and death are not synonyms for being and nonbeing, but two kinds of existence. Essentially, death is separation; the soul is physically separated from the body, the person is spiritually separated from God. Death itself is the passage from one kind of existence to another. Our individual consciousness continues, but in a new place and condition.

All humans fear death—the result of Adam's sin (Romans 5:15,17-18; 6:23; 1 Corinthians 15:22). But death makes its presence known long before we approach the end of our earthly years. We constantly live in a state of spiritual death until we believe in Christ. Likewise, the reality of physical death rests on

94

LAST THINGS

our minds regardless of temporary distractions we pursue (Hebrews 2:15).

The Bible's central message is that Christ died but defeated death by returning to life (1 Corinthians 15:3-4). Because He conquered death and the Devil who controlled it, we know He holds the power of death in His own hands (Hebrews 2:14-15; Revelation 1:17-18). As a result, Christ can and does give us eternal life, and our eternal life doesn't wait for physical death before it begins. At the point anyone believes in Him, "he has crossed over from death to life" (John 5:24). Even though Christians still die physically, death can never separate us from Him who died for us (Romans 8:38-39). As a result, Christians regard physical death as a benefit—the means by which we come into Christ's immediate presence (Philippians 1:21).

Discussion of death raises the issue of the time between physical death and the resurrection of the body. The Bible states that we enter the Lord's presence at the moment of death (Philippians 1:23; 2 Corinthians 5:8). Nonbiblical alternate views hold that there is an intermediate state, either purgatory or soul sleep. Purgatory is an alleged place of purging of sins (punishment) after we die but before we enter heaven. This view contradicts the sufficiency of Christ's death, which fully paid for our sins (Hebrews 9:26; 10:2,10). Soul sleep is the notion that the dead exist in an unconscious state until the resurrection. But Jesus told the thief on the cross, "Today you will be with me in paradise" (Luke 23:43). Proponents of purgatory and soul sleep try to back up their views with Scripture, but the majority of Protestant Christians disagree with their interpretations.

Christ's death and resurrection have removed death's power and curse. So when our Christian loved ones die, we don't "grieve like the rest of men, who have no hope" (1 Thessalonians 4:13). Because of Christ's triumph over death, we can grieve but retain our confidence, knowing we already have eternal life in Him. We anticipate death as merely the transition from this life to the full experience of our life with Christ forever.

The Final Exam

God's judgment reflects His character. Because He is just, He must judge. As Creator He has the right, the ability, and the inclination to judge, and He does. He made humans in His image—with moral sensibility—and we must give an account. So God rightly holds us accountable. According to Jesus, the ultimate basis of judgment is one's relationship to Himself (Luke 12:8-9). Anyone might claim that relationship, but our works provide the evidence that our claim is real. "As the body without the spirit is dead, so faith without deeds is dead" (James 2:26). "Works" and "deeds" are commonly used to describe the actions we take to accomplish God's will—helping the lost and the needy, practicing spiritual disciplines, and treating others with love.

As in much of theology, scholars hold different views about future judgment. Some believe in one final judgment for all people from all time, lost and saved alike. Others believe in a series of judgments interspersed among the end time events for various individuals and groups.

95 LAST THINGS

307

Some believe Christians will undergo a judgment separate from nonbelievers to hear Christ's assessment of their works. "For we must all appear before the judgment seat of Christ, that each one may receive what is due him for the things done while in the body, whether good or bad" (2 Corinthians 5:10). Our destiny is not the issue "since we have been justified through faith, [and] have peace with God through our Lord Jesus Christ" (Romans 5:1). Neither will our sin be judged because it was already judged in Christ, and "there is now no condemnation for those who are in Christ Jesus" (Romans 8:1). But we will lose rewards in heaven for works that fail to pass Jesus' scrutiny (1 Corinthians 3:14-15).

Jesus, Paul, Peter, and James used heavenly rewards as incentives in this life (Matthew 10:41-42; 2 Timothy 4:8; 1 Peter 5:4; James 1:12). We should earn all we can, aware that we can lose them too. Like Paul in 1 Corinthians 3:15, John says we can lose rewards. "Watch out that you do not lose what you have worked for, but that you may be rewarded fully" (2 John 1:8). The Bible doesn't describe the exact nature of these rewards, but they are earned or lost through a godly life, including motives as well as actions.

The Final Judgment will be based on two sets of books (Revelation 20:11-15). The lost will be judged according to their human works found in "the books." That record of their lives offers evidence that they did not believe in Jesus Christ, the Lamb of God who takes away the sin of the world. By their deeds, all will see the convicting proof of their lost state. The saved will be judged out of "The Book of Life," a list of all who accepted God's mercy through Christ who died for them.

God's judgment should not be taken lightly. The Bible's message of grace is set against the backdrop of a just God before whom we live. Receiving His mercy by faith alone is the only way to avoid His eternal judgment. Christians are spared by Christ's sacrificial mercy on our behalf, and His promise of rewards or their potential loss should motivate us to live for Him who forgave our sin. Human history is moving toward a goal—God's glory. His objective is to glorify Himself, and He will do it through both grace and judgment.

Utopia

Most people long for a perfect world. They define it differently and follow diverse paths to find it, but they dream of utopia where justice reigns and evil is subdued. "Fat chance," the cynic cries. But the cynic usually reflects the bitterness of his own dream for a perfect society, now lost, crushed by mankind's repeated failures. The Bible records such a world—a perfect order built on the twin pillars of justice and righteousness— that will occur sometime in the future. Exactly when this utopia will arrive and how it will look is the source of great speculation and debate among Christians.

Christians speak of "The Millennium," from the Latin word for a thousand, referring to a state of harmony on earth (Revelation 20:1-6). The Millennium is understood by Christians in different ways, related to the timing of Christ's return. As the name suggests, premillennialism anticipates His return before the Millennium. Postmillennialism believes He will return afterward. Amillennialism does not envision a literal thousand-year reign of Christ. Let's consider each of these positions.

The premillennial view expects catastrophic global upheaval as the sign of Christ's visible, sudden return. He will establish a literal, visible thousand-year reign of truth and righteousness during which He will rule the world with His saints. Premillennialism also believes that many Jews will come to Christ just prior to the Millennium, and it will therefore have a largely Jewish flavor. Satan will be locked up and the curse of the Fall will be revoked (Romans 8:19-23), resulting in a golden age.

The postmillennial perspective looks at the present more than the future. The current spread of the gospel and Christian teaching will gradually improve society until nearly complete conversion occurs. Evil will be significantly reduced as Christian morality increasingly influences the world. This time of worldwide Christianization will not necessarily be a literal one thousand years because that number is considered symbolic. Christ will return at the end of that time.

Amillennialism does not hold to a literal reign of Christ, but believes good and evil will simultaneously spread until He comes back. This view holds that the kingdom of God is now present as Christ rules His church, thus the Millennium is being experienced by the church right now. Biblical passages about a future, perfect world refer to the new heaven and earth.

Amillennialism sees most prophesy as symbolic and considers it fulfilled in past history rather than coming in the future.

The church's view of the Millennium has shifted throughout history. During the first three centuries, premillennialism was dominant. Amillennialism was more widespread into the Middle Ages. The Reformers focused on more urgent areas of theology in their historical context, and were cautious about excess millennial theorizing. The premillennial view experienced a resurgence in the seventeenth century, while postmillennial interest grew in the eighteenth. All three positions are found today.

Whatever view one believes has the best biblical support, they share a common central theme—Jesus Christ has won the conflict over evil. He will return and usher in a perfect eternity—a utopia in which God and His people will enjoy one another forever. The forces of evil, satanic or human, do not and cannot defeat the Son of God. Jesus Christ wins, and in Him we win too.

Snatched Away

The wildly popular *Left Behind* series by Tim LaHaye and Jerry Jenkins (Tyndale) is built around the "Rapture." The word refers to the return of Christ to remove His followers from earth at the end of this age—a moment in time when all believers on earth will instantaneously disappear. The central passage is 1 Thessalonians 4:15-17:

> [W]e who are still alive, who are left till the coming of the Lord, will certainly not precede those who have fallen asleep. For the Lord himself will come down from heaven, with a loud command, with the voice of the archangel and with the trumpet call of God, and the dead in Christ will rise first. After that, we who are still alive and are left will be caught up together with them in the clouds to meet the Lord in the air.

The Rapture is a doctrine held almost exclusively by premillennialists, and it's understood differently even among them. The dividing issue is whether the Rapture

97 LAST THINGS

313

occurs before, during, or after the Tribulation—seven years of God's judgment on the human race. The timing of the Rapture determines if the church will undergo that awful ordeal or avoid it.

The pretribulation position anticipates Christ's return to deliver the church before God's judgment comes. Christ won't come all the way to the earth—believers will be caught up to meet the Lord who will take them to heaven for the seven years of Tribulation. This requires belief in the Rapture's imminency, found, it is believed, in Titus 2:13: "We wait for the blessed hope—the glorious appearing of our great God and Savior, Jesus Christ." If we must go through the Tribulation before the Rapture, we wouldn't be waiting for it, but anticipating seven years of hell on earth, hardly a "blessed hope."

The posttribulation view believes the Lord will return after the Tribulation. This means God will not remove the church, but preserve it through that terrible time. This position interprets 1 Thessalonians 4:15-17 as the church meeting the Lord to immediately return to earth with Him to set up His millennial kingdom. In other words, Christ raptures His saints and sets up His reign in one step. The blessed hope is our trust in God's protection in the midst of the Tribulation. Biblical instruction for the church about the last days is pointless if the church doesn't experience those times.

Trying to blend the best of both views, some Christians choose a middle path, believing in a midtribulation Rapture. As the name implies, Christ will return to remove His church in the middle of the Tribulation, before the worst begins when God's full wrath is poured out on the earth. Advocates emphasize the Bible's several references to three and a half years (Daniel 9; 12; Revelation 11; 12). They believe that period of time indicates a significant break at the midpoint of the Tribulation when Christ returns to remove His church.

This doctrine is an example of where Christians should tolerate differences on less-than-essential issues. The Lord will return whenever He chooses, and all true believers will be included in His victory. Only God knows when that will be, but we can agree on the most important issue—Christ will come back and He will rule. Together we can praise Him for His victory.

The Ultimate Bad Guy

No one wants a license plate or street address with the number 666, the symbol of the Antichrist (Revelation 13:18). Mention the Antichrist and people recall their favorite horror movie or imagine Adolf Hitler or joke about their seventh-grade English teacher. The title has become a synonym for whoever or whatever represents ultimate evil.

The word "antichrist" itself appears in the Bible only five times, all in John's letters. It means "against Christ," and can be used in a general sense for anyone who denies the true Christ. The common use is for the end-times figure who will try to establish himself as the counterfeit Christ to entice people into following him.

First John 4:3 records that the spirit of the Antichrist is found in those who do not acknowledge that Jesus is from God. The apostle also says that anyone who denies that Jesus Christ has come in the flesh is the deceiver and the Antichrist (2 John 7). John is probably referring to early heretics who denied Christ's physical humanity, claiming He only seemed to be human. Even

98

LAST THINGS

though John says "many antichrists" were present in his time, he warns that the final Antichrist was yet to come (1 John 2:18; 4:3). Paul calls him "the man of lawlessness" (2 Thessalonians 2:3) who "will oppose and will exalt himself over everything that is called God or is worshiped, so that he sets himself up in God's temple, proclaiming himself to be God" (2 Thessalonians 2:4).

In Revelation, John portrays the Antichrist as "the beast" (Revelation 13:1-18; 17:7-17), the satanically empowered forgery of the real Christ. His blend of terror and enticement will be so overwhelming that "all inhabitants of the earth will worship the beast—all whose names have not been written in the book of life belonging to the Lamb that was slain from the creation of the world" (Revelation 13:8). Revelation 13:3 says "his fatal wound had been healed," causing speculation that he may effect a counterfeit resurrection astonishing the whole world, resulting in their worshiping him.

Christians through the ages have tried to identify the Antichrist within their own time. Men of unequaled authority and terror, especially those who persecuted the church, ranked high on the list of prime suspects. One of the earliest was Nero. The fourth century archheretic Arius, who denied the deity of Christ, was also considered. In the sixteenth century, the reformers and

Protestants persecuted by the Roman Catholic Church viewed the pope as the Antichrist. Adolf Hitler probably gets the most votes in recent times.

All past attempts to identify the Antichrist have failed. Even the worst historical figures don't match the grizzly deeds of the end-times tyrant. The spirit of Antichrist dwells upon the earth even now, wreaking havoc and opposing God and His people, but the worst is yet to come. This satanic force will be personified during the end times. Nevertheless, despite his temporary success, he will not prevail. The Son of God will return to conquer and judge (2 Thessalonians 2:8-9; Revelation 19:11-16).

The Worst Nightmare

One line from a Newsboys' song reminds us that—"They don't serve breakfast in hell." Our society largely disbelieves in hell, but people still describe their worst suffering as "hell on earth." No one really knows what hell is like, but we picture our terrible situations in the most graphic words possible, usually some comparison to hell. The idea of hell is so ghastly it's hard to believe someone just made it up. But the Bible says a lot about it, mostly in the words of Jesus Himself.

The Scriptures sometimes use the word "hell" for the grave or the place of the dead. But the common meaning is the eternal punishment for those who reject God and His grace. Jesus portrayed it as "darkness, where there will be weeping and gnashing of teeth" (Matthew 8:12) and a place of fire and punishment (Matthew 25:41,46).

The images of hell may be symbolic, but if they are, the realities are worse than the symbols. Perhaps the worst part is that hell lasts forever. John the Baptist called it "unquenchable fire" (Matthew 3:12). Jesus referred to it as "eternal" (Matthew 25:41,46), and

99 LAST THINGS

specified that "the fire never goes out" and "is not quenched" (Mark 9:43,48). Paul said it's "everlasting" in 2 Thessalonians 1:9. In addition to physical agony, hell's occupants experience unrelenting guilt and regret. They will know they rejected God's offer of mercy in Christ, resulting in separation from Him and everything holy, good, and beautiful.

Some people believe in universalism, the idea that everyone will eventually be saved. But Jesus' words seem unmistakable: "Then they will go away to *eternal* punishment, but the righteous to *eternal* life" (Matthew 25:46, emphasis added). While some point to God's incomparable grace to suggest there may be "second chances" of which we're unaware, no second chance after death is implied in Scripture. To the contrary, "Man is destined to die once, and after that to face judgment" (Hebrews 9:27). Others propose annihilationism, the belief that the wicked are exterminated immediately at death or after some temporary punishment. They then no longer exist at all. But the Bible's many references to eternal hell argue against that view.

Hell is terrible, but not unfair. God honors peoples' rejection of His love, and He gives them what they want—His absence. Because of sin everyone deserves hell, including both those who accept God's offer of rescue through Christ and those who refuse it. God wants no one there: "He is patient with you, not wanting anyone to perish, but everyone to come to repentance" (2 Peter 3:9). No one goes to hell unjustly. The perfect judge of the universe does not err in even one case—no one is in hell by mistake.

As horrifying as the doctrine of hell is, one benefit is our increased gratitude for God's mercy and grace and forgiveness. It also reminds us how important life decisions are—they affect our future destiny. Our passion for evangelism is heightened by knowing the eternal outcome for those who don't know Christ. May this doctrine sober us enough to do God's work with great passion.

99 | LAST THINGS

The Perfect Dream

Heaven is primarily God's presence and the blessings that flow from Him. Good is abundant and evil absent. God's people from all time and every nation will fellowship with one another and their loved ones in perfect harmony, with no pain, suffering, tears, death, or grief (Revelation 21:3-4). We will forever share pure, complete joy and love in the presence of our Redeemer Jesus Christ. But several questions arise about heaven's space and time and our memory and activity there.

Is heaven a physical place or a state of being? Because Jesus' resurrection body was a glorified *physical* body, and it ascended into heaven (Acts 1:9), it must be some*where*, implying that heaven is a place. Our resurrection bodies will also be physical, likewise demanding the need to be some*where*. On the other hand, heaven is communion with the immaterial, omnipresent Spirit, neither physical nor localized in one place, implying that heaven is a state of being. So heaven is probably both a place and a state of being.

Since heaven is life in God's presence, do we enter

God's timeless realm? Revelation 22:2 says the tree of life yields fruit *every month.* That imagery may be symbolic, but since this tree of life parallels the tree of life in the garden (Genesis 2:9; 3:22; 3:24), which was literal, it would seem that "every month" refers to literal time. Furthermore, since we don't become omnipresent or omniscient like God, we can't presume that we'll become timeless like God.

Will we remember this life and recognize our loved ones? Whatever memory of earthly life we'll possess, it will exclude our sins and failures and anything resulting in sadness, sorrow, or pain (Revelation 21:4). Not recognizing our loved ones seems out of character with heaven's maximum joy. Peter accurately identified Moses and Elijah at Jesus' transfiguration (Matthew 17:3-4). That event was not exactly a glimpse of heaven, but it reveals recognizable personal factors after death. We will apparently obtain at least partial memory in heaven.

What will we do in heaven? Our time will include rest, but we will not be inactive. Our rest is pictured in Hebrews 4:9-10: "There remains, then, a Sabbath-rest for the people of God; for anyone who enters God's rest also rests from his own work, just as God did from his." Revelation 19:6-7 describes worship: "I heard what sounded like a great multitude, like the roar of rushing waters and like loud peals of thunder, shouting: 'Hallelujah! For our Lord God Almighty reigns. Let us rejoice and be glad and give him glory!'" We will also serve. In Jesus' parable about service, the results of faithfulness depict eternity, and the good servant will be put "in charge of many things" (Matthew 25:20-21), a clear picture of active service.

Those heavenly benefits have already begun. We rest now, knowing that our eternal destiny is safe in Christ, protected by His incomparable power. We also worship now, both when we gather to corporately praise God, and in our hearts with our attitude of adoration. And we serve now, striving to do everything for His glory. Our official home is heaven even now because our citizenship is already registered there (Philippians 3:20). We are just awaiting the final transfer.

APPENDIX A

Index of Topics

Recommended Books

Clowney, E. P. *The Church.* Downers Grove, Ill.: InterVarsity, 1995.

Couch, M. *A Biblical Theology of the Church.* Grand Rapids, Mich.: Kregel, 1999.

Demarest, B. "Systematic Theology." In *Evangelical Dictionary of Theology.* Grand Rapids, Mich.: Baker, 1984.

Demarest, B. *The Cross and Salvation.* Wheaton, Ill.: Crossway, 1997.

Elwell, W. A. Ed. *Evangelical Dictionary of Theology.* Grand Rapids, Mich.: Baker, 1984.

Elwell, W. A., Ed. *Baker Encyclopedia of the Bible.* Grand Rapids, Mich.: Baker, 1988.

Erickson, M. J. *Christian Theology.* Grand Rapids, Mich.: Baker, 1983.

Erickson, M. J. *Introducing Christian Doctrine.* L. A. Hustad, Ed. Grand Rapids, Mich.: Baker, 1992.

Geisler, N. L. "Epistemology." In *Baker Encyclopedia of Christian Apologetics.* Grand Rapids, Mich.: Baker, 1999.

Getz, G. A. *Sharpening the Focus of the Church*. Chicago, Ill.: Moody Press, 1974.

Green, J. B., McKnight, S. & Marshall, I. H. Eds. *Dictionary of Jesus and the Gospels*. Downers Grove, Ill.: InterVarsity, 1992.

Grenz, S. J., & Olson, R. E. *Who Needs Theology: An Invitation to the Study of God*. Downers Grove, Ill.: InterVarsity, 1996.

Grudem, W. *Systematic Theology: An Introduction to Biblical Doctrine*. Grand Rapids, Mich.: Zondervan, 1994.

Hawthorne, G. F., Martin, R. P., & Reid, D. G. Eds. *Dictionary of Paul and His Letters*. Downers Grove, Ill.: InterVarsity, 1993.

Klein, W. W., Blomberg, C. L., & Hubbard, Jr., R. L. *Introduction to Biblical Interpretation*. Dallas, Tex.: Word, 1993.

Letham, R. *The Work of Christ*. Downers Grove, Ill.: InterVarsity, 1993.

Lewis, G. R. & Demarest, B. A. *Integrative Theology*. Grand Rapids, Mich.: Zondervan, 1987, 1990, 1994.

Packer, J. I. *Concise Theology: A Guide to Historic Christian Beliefs*. Wheaton, Ill.: Tyndale, 1993.

Packer, J. I. *Keep in Step with the Spirit*. Old Tappan, N.J.: Revell, 1984.

Ryrie, C. C. *Basic Theology: A Popular Systematic Guide to Understanding Biblical Truth.* Wheaton, Ill.: Victor, 1987.

Shelley, B. L. *What Is the Church?* Wheaton, Ill.: Victor, 1978.

Sproul, R. C. *Essential Truths of the Christian Faith.* Wheaton, Ill.: Tyndale, 1992.

Thrasher, W. L. *Basics for Believers: Foundational Truths to Guide Your Life.* Chicago, Ill.: Moody, 1998, 2000.

Unger. M. F. *The New Unger's Bible Dictionary* (revised and updated). Chicago, Ill.: Moody, 1988.

Wegner, P. D. *The Journey from Texts to Translations: The Origin and Development of the Bible.* Grand Rapids, Mich.: Baker, 1999.

Notes

1. G. R. Lewis & B. A. Demarest, *Integrative Theology*, vol. 1. (Grand Rapids, Mich.: Zondervan, 1987), pp. 25-26.

2. M. J. Erickson, *Christian Theology* (Grand Rapids, Mich.: Baker, 1983), pp. 79-80.

3. W. Grudem, *Systematic Theology: An Introduction to Biblical Doctrine* (Grand Rapids, Mich.: Zondervan, 1994), p. 563.

4. Erickson, pp. 263, 283.

5. J. P. Moreland, *Love Your God with All Your Mind* (Colorado Springs: NavPress, 1997).

6. Grudem, p. 563.

7. Erickson, p. 736.

Author

Dr. Rick Cornish is senior pastor of First Baptist Church in Luverne, Minnesota. He has also pastored in Kansas and Wyoming, and previously taught New Testament and Systematic Theology for seven years in the former Soviet Union. A graduate of Denver Seminary, Rick lives in Minnesota with his wife, Tracy, and their two sons Scott and Ben—the original and most important audience for this book.

Check out these other great titles in the 5 Minute Series!